92

SANTA ANA PUBLIC LIBRARY

D0461649

SANTA ANA PUBLIC LIBRARY

SANTA ANA PUBLIC LIBRARY

SANTA ANA PUBLIC LIBRARY

YA
970.4
AND

018.95

The First Americans

❖•❖•❖•❖•❖•❖•❖•❖•❖

INDIANS OF THE PLAINS

Elaine Andrews

YA 970.4 AND
Andrews, Elaine K.
Indians of the Plains
31994007926410

Facts On File
New York • Oxford

SANTA ANA PUBLIC LIBRARY

About *The First Americans* Series:

This eight-volume series presents the rich and varied cultures of the many Native American tribes, placing each within its geographical and historical context. Each volume covers a different cultural area, providing an understanding of all the major North American Indian tribes in a systematic, region-by-region survey. The series emphasizes the contributions of Native Americans to American culture, illustrating their legacy in striking photographs within the text and in all-color photo essays.

Indians of the Plains

Copyright © 1992 by Benford Books, Inc.

All rights reserved. No part of this book may be reproduced or utilized in any form or by any means, electronic or mechanical, including photocopying, recording, or by any information storage or retrieval systems, without permission in writing from the publisher. For information contact:

Facts On File, Inc.
460 Park Avenue South
New York NY 10016
USA

Facts On File Limited
Collins Street
Oxford OX4 1XJ
United Kingdom

Library of Congress Cataloging-in-Publication Data

Andrews, Elaine K.
    Indians of the Plains / Elaine Andrews
        p.   cm. — The First Americans series
    Includes index.
    Summary: Examines the history, culture, changing fortunes, and
current situation of the various Indian peoples of the Great Plains region.
    ISBN 0-8160-2387-5
    1. Indians of North America—Great Plains—Juvenile literature.
[1. Indians of North America—Great Plains.]
I. Title   II. Series.
E78.G73A53   1991
978'.00497—dc20   90–45545

A British CIP catalogue record for this book is available from the British Library.

Facts On File books are available at special discounts when purchased in bulk quantities for businesses, associations, institutions or sales promotions. Please call our Special Sales Department in New York at 212/683-2244 (dial 800/322-8755 except in NY, AK or HI) or in Oxford at 865/728399.

Design by Carmela Pereira
Jacket design by Donna Sinisgalli
Typography & composition by Tony Meisel
Manufactured in MEXICO

10 9 8 7 6 5 4 3 2 1

This book is printed on acid-free paper.

▲ Crow men were noted for their long hair. This photo, taken around 1867, is of a Crow who acted as a scout for the U.S. Army.

CONTENTS

❖ • ❖ • ❖ • ❖ • ❖ • ❖ • ❖ • ❖ • ❖ • ❖ • ❖

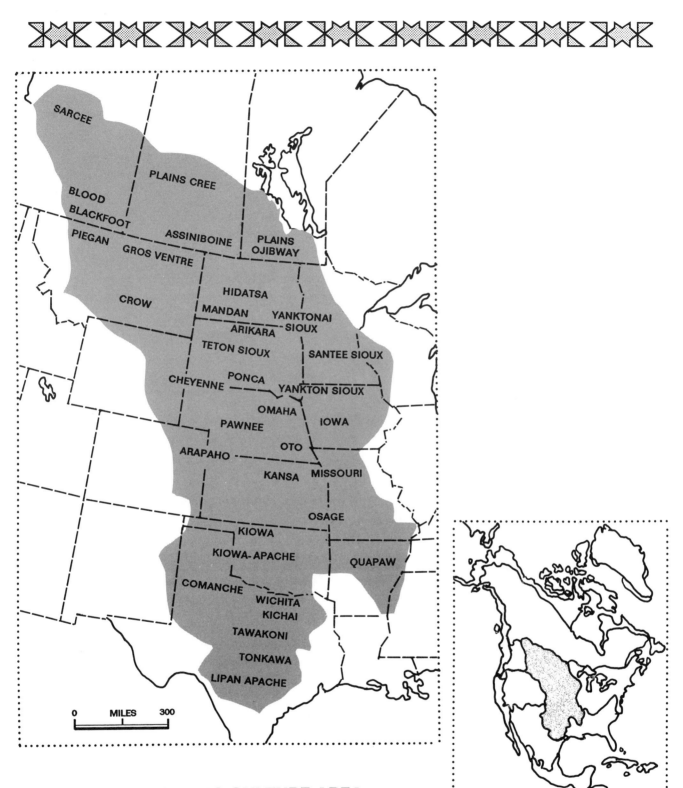

THE PLAINS CULTURE AREA

The approximate traditional tribal boundaries of the Plains culture area are shown in the larger map, with modern state boundaries. The smaller map shows the culture area in relation to all of North America.

▲ Sleeping Bull, a Blackfoot, wears his warrior outfit. His hair is tied into the typical Blackfoot knot on his forehead. The sword he carries was not a traditional Indian weapon. It could have been a trophy of the Indian wars, taken from an army cavalry soldier.

CHAPTER ONE

❖ • ❖ • ❖ • ❖ • ❖ • ❖ • ❖ • ❖ • ❖ • ❖ • ❖

ROOTS

Often, when people think about the Indians of the Plains, they conjure up an image of a warrior clad in buckskins astride a spotted pony. He wears an elegant headdress whose feathers stream down his back, and brandishes a lance decked with human scalps. His face is painted for war. Or he may be a half-naked hunter with bow and arrows plunging his pony into a herd of panicked buffalo.

Many Indians living on the Plains were indeed warriors who fiercely defended their lands from encroaching settlers. Tribes also fought with one another over territory, for horses, and in retaliation for raids. As skilled hunters, Indians pursued the buffalo across the Plains.

There the stereotype ends. For although the Plains Indians descended from a common origin (as did all Native Americans), they were many different peoples. Each group had its own culture, language, beliefs, and history. Many were farmers who lived in villages along the rivers and ventured onto the high Plains to hunt only once a year. Other farming groups shared the Plains with the hunters, who moved across the rolling grasslands in search of buffalo.

Some lived in villages of tepees, which could be easily dismantled and carried by dogs or horses as the entire village moved from place to place to hunt. Others lived in more permanent villages whose lodges were made of earth, grass, or skin. Their artifacts, clothing, adornments, and their hairstyles reflected their differences.

The Indians of the Plains spoke several different languages and dialects. But they communicated through a sign language of gestures that all tribes could understand. Their beliefs, myths, stories, and ceremonies often differed from tribe to tribe.

Most experts agree that the Plains Indians with which we are familiar are descendants of Indian groups east of the Mississippi River who, over centuries, migrated westward. They settled onto the vast open spaces of the Plains and adapted their way of life to the new environment they found there.

LANDSCAPE OF THE PLAINS

From the Mississippi River west to the Rocky Mountains, from Canada's Saskatchewan River south into central Texas, the Plains of North America form the heartland of the continent. This vast expanse of flat, windswept prairies and gently rolling hills is essentially a grassland.

Geographers generally divide the Plains into the eastern region, or the prairies, and the west-

ern portion, or the Great Plains. The prairies are the American Middle West, reaching from the Mississippi to about the middle of the "prairie" states—the Dakotas, Nebraska, Kansas, the northern parts of Texas. Once characterized as "a sea of grass," the prairies were known for the tender green grass, which often grew as tall as 10 feet. Before settlers plowed the soil into farmland, built roads, and settled into towns, the tall-grass prairie covered some 400,000 square miles.

Extending westward to the Rocky Mountains, the land slopes gently upward to form the Great Plains. Here the grass is shorter and tougher. These high Plains, or steppes, were home to the seemingly endless herds of buffalo that grazed where cattle and wheat now thrive.

The climate in both the prairies and the Plains is scorching in the summer and bitter cold in winter. The prairies are more humid, with about 20 inches of rainfall a year. Rainfall in the Great Plains is scant and undependable. It may range from 15 inches a year to less than 4 inches. Drought and dustbowls are common in parts of the Great Plains.

In the early 19th century, Americans characterized much of the Plains area as the Great American Desert. They thought of it as a dry, waterless area. Much of the high Plains is dry, but it

▲ In 1833 the artist Karl Bodmer captured this scene of a Mandan village perched high on bluffs overlooking the upper Missouri River in North Dakota. The women in the foreground are launching small, round boats called bull-boats made of willow branches covered with buffalo hide.

is not waterless. One of North America's largest river systems winds through the Plains. Rising in the Rocky Mountains, the broad Missouri is the longest river in the United States. Flowing for more than 2,500 miles, it courses across the northern Plains and then flows south through the central Plains to join the Mississippi River. Along with its tributaries—the Platte, the Kansas, the James, the Yellowstone, the Bighorn—the Missouri forms the major river system of the northern and central Plains.

The Arkansas River with its tributaries, the great Red River, the White River, the Ouchita, and other smaller rivers drain the southern Plains. These rivers all form part of the vast Mississippi River System.

Compared to the great forests of the eastern and western regions of North America, the Plains and prairies are treeless, but not quite. Willows, cottonwoods, and oaks grow in the river valleys

▲ This panorama of the great camp of the Piegan, who gathered their tepees on the plains of northern Montana for the buffalo-hunting season, was painted by Karl Bodmer in the 1830s. The Piegan were a subdivision of the Blackfoot people.

of the prairies. Even though many streams and rivers in the Great Plains are dry in summer, willows and cottonwoods survive along their meandering banks.

ANIMALS OF THE PLAINS

As the natural landscape of prairies and Plains has shrunk with the growth and the industrialization of the United States, so too the amount of wildlife has decreased. The unsettled grasslands once abounded with animals. Most famous were the buffalo—huge, cattlelike beasts with short horns and heavy, humped shoulders. Enormous herds of buffalo grazed the short grasses of the

Plains from Canada into Texas, migrating south in winter and north in summer. The largest bulls might measure six feet high at the shoulders and weigh as much as a ton each. Since they were neither swift runners nor gifted with good eyesight, they were easy prey for the Indians and later for European hunters with guns. Before they were nearly wiped out by hunters slaughtering them for meat and hides, it is estimated that 60,000,000 buffalo wandered the Plains.

Sharing the grasslands with the buffalo were some 40,000,000 pronghorns, relatives of the antelope. About the size of a large goat, with prongs on their horns, these animals were the swiftest on the Plains. To escape predators, they could run 40 miles an hour.

Outnumbering the buffalo and the pronghorns combined were the black-tailed prairie dogs. The explorers Lewis and Clark called them "barking squirrels." No one knows exactly how many of these burrowing rodents lived on the Plains, but some estimate their numbers in the hundreds of

▲ The vast buffalo herds that once covered the Plains gave the Indians their food, clothing, and shelter.

millions. They tunneled under the soil, digging up the dirt into mounds that marked the entrances to their burrows. While one group of prairie dogs foraged in the grasses, another stood guard at the burrow entrance. When danger approached, in the form of a falcon or prairie ferret, the sentries barked the alarm, and they all scuttled into the burrows.

The Plains were also the home of countless other animals. The chief predators were wolves, coyotes, cougars, and bobcats, as well as birds—hawks, eagles, owls. Deer and elk grazed the Plains along with jackrabbits and bears, and beavers made their homes in the rivers and along the streams.

INDIAN ORIGINS

Scientists believe that during the Ice Age that ended about 10,000 years ago, the first inhabitants of the Americas migrated from Asia across a land bridge that once connected Alaska with Siberia. However, they do not agree as to when these nomadic hunters first made this journey. Some believe that people inhabited an area in Alaska as early as 27,000 B.C. Others argue that there is not enough archaeological evidence to prove such an early date. Still other experts believe that further research will uncover the presence of people as early as 70,000 B.C.

Most experts will agree, however, that by 18,000 years ago, hunters had crossed the land bridge and occupied what is now the Yukon re-

gion of Alaska. At that time, the land bridge, which is known as Beringia, was a grassland some 1,000 miles wide. During this same period, the entire northern half of North America was encased in glacial ice. However, because so little moisture exists in the part of the Arctic that encompassed Beringia, the land bridge escaped the ice. Over the millennia, as the climate warmed and the seas rose from the melting glaciers, Beringia disappeared. It is now submerged under the waters of the Bering Strait.

Asian hunters followed the trails of the big game along the grasslands of Beringia and into North America. Their prey were giant bison, mammoths, mastodons, musk oxen, and caribou. Animal predators, such as saber-toothed tigers, lions, giant wolves, bears, and even cheetahs, followed the migration of the big game animals.

Most scholars agree that the hunters, who traveled in bands with women and children, were "modern" people who were physically very like people today. Archaeological evidence indicates that their brains were full size, and experts believe they had a spoken language. They used spears tipped with stone or bone, and they fashioned tools such as knives and hide scrapers from animal bones. There is evidence that they used spear throwers powerful enough to thrust a spear through a mammoth's thick hide and deep into its body. The animals they killed provided

▲ This painting of a Mandan lodge shows how roomy a dwelling could be. The roof hole let smoke out and light in. The spears in the foreground are similar to those made centuries earlier by ancestors of the Indians.

them with all their needs—skins for clothing and shelter, meat for food, and bones for weapons and tools.

Following the herds of grazing animals, the hunters slowly spread into the interior of the Americas. There is no conclusive proof to determine how they made their way over the ice sheet that spread 1,000 miles southward into North America. Some experts think they followed the big game through ice-free valleys that existed along the edge of the eastern Rockies. Others believe they took a route through ice-free areas along the Pacific coast. Whatever their route, the great ice sheet had melted by 11,000 years ago, and the descendants of the Asian hunters had expanded into North America, Mexico, and South America.

In North America, archaeologists have excavated sites from coast to coast. They have uncovered carefully crafted spear points of bone and stone, tools of bone, charcoal from fires, and the remains of animals long extinct. In Mexico and South America, they have found thousands of similar artifacts, indicating the presence of humans. Archaeologists do not always agree on the precise dates of their finds, but they do conclude that as the Ice Age came to an end the first Americans were firmly established on both continents.

FROM HUNTERS TO FARMERS

Over hundreds of years, as humans advanced into the Americas, the great animals of the Ice Age began to disappear. Mastodons, mammoths, camels, lions, sloths, saber-toothed tigers, giant bears, and horses eventually vanished from the continent. Scientists have different theories about how these animals became extinct. Some argue that the hunters were so efficient that they exterminated the big game. Others contend that the tremendous climate changes signaling the end of the Ice Age so changed the animals' habitat that they could no longer survive. Both events probably coincided to cause the extinction. Weakened by violent environmental change, the animals were easy prey for skilled hunters.

As the largest animals disappeared, the hunters learned to rely on smaller game—rabbits, deer, birds—and on fish and shellfish. They also began to gather wild plants. Slowly, over the centuries, the nomadic hunters became farmers and settled on the land. From their observations of how plants grow in the wild, they learned to raise these plants themselves. Pumpkins, squash, beans, potatoes, tomatoes, and peanuts were cultivated. Perhaps their most important crop was maize, which today is called corn.

Most experts believe that farming began in Central and South America, possibly around 10,000 years ago. Planting and cultivating crops forced the people to stay close to their fields; and so they began to settle in permanent communities. With a more plentiful and reliable supply of food, their populations increased. They often had

▲ This young Mandan man wears a buffalo robe. He played the flute he carries when he courted a woman to be his wife.

a surplus of food, which gave them more time to develop their cultures. Slowly the great civilizations of the Maya, Toltec, and Inca grew in Central and South America.

From the south, farming spread into North America. Farming in what is now the United States first took root in the Southwest and Southeast. The ruins left by the Pueblo people of the Southwest show that they farmed extensively, built elaborate stone dwellings, created beautiful objects such as pottery and jewelry, and had an organized social system.

It is believed that the farming culture of the Southeast spread from Mexico along the Gulf coast into the Mississippi Valley as far north as the Great Lakes. The fertile land gave an abundance, and even a surplus, of food. With time for

work other than farming, the people created beautiful works of art and architecture. These early southeastern people are most famous for the huge earthen mounds they built as religious symbols and as burial sites. Known as the "mound builders," these people traded extensively with one another, carrying their products and their knowledge of farming over the region. With their passing, farming spread, moving eastward toward the Atlantic Ocean, northward into Canada, and westward onto the prairies.

PEOPLE OF THE PLAINS

Archaeological finds of spear points, stone tools, and animal bones indicate that prehistoric hunters lived on the western Plains at least 10,000 years ago. Slowly but steadily, as farming spread westward, the Indians of the east replaced these people. Eastern Indians occupied the grasslands of the prairies west of the Mississippi and eventually moved onto the Great Plains.

Historians often classify the Indians of the

PLAINS LANGUAGES

The different tribes of the Plains spoke numerous different languages, but some languages were related to each other. People who spoke one language in a language family could usually understand people who spoke another language in the same family. Sometimes, however, the differences were such that they had to communicate in sign language. There were seven major language families among the Plains Indians. The chart below gives the language families and the tribes who spoke each language.

ATHAPASCAN
Kiowa-Apache
Lipan Apache
Sarcee

CADDOAN
Arikara
Pawnee
Wichita

KIOWA-TANOAN
Kiowa

SIOUAN
Assiniboine
Crow
Hidatsa
Iowa
Kansa
Mandan
Missouri
Omaha
Osage
Oto
Ponca
Quapaw
Sioux

ALGONQUIAN
Arapaho
Blackfoot
Cheyenne
Gros Ventre
Plains Cree
Plains Ojibway

TONKAWAN
Tonkawa

UTO-AZTEC
Comanche

Plains into two groups—the farming-hunting tribes of the prairies, and the tribes of the Great Plains who moved from place to place hunting buffalo. They further classify groups according to language families.

PRAIRIE FARMER–HUNTERS

The tribes discussed below are the major tribes of the prairies.

Arikara

The Arikara lived along the Missouri River in what is now North Dakota. Primarily farmers, they also hunted small game and some buffalo. A Caddoan-speaking people, they migrated from the southeast into Texas and through the central Plains into North Dakota.

Kansa

A Siouan-speaking people, the Kansa, also called the Kaw, had migrated from east of the Mississippi to Kansas, settling along the Kansas River. A peaceful people, they lived in farming villages and occasionally went onto the high Plains to hunt buffalo.

Mandan

Villagers and farmers, the Mandan lived along the upper Missouri River in what is now North Dakota, often building their villages on the high bluffs of the river. Like other farming tribes, they hunted buffalo in the summer and traded with other tribes. Although they lived in the same area as the Arikara, the Mandan were Siouan people.

Osage

The Osage, a people of Siouan origin, were recognized by whites and other Indian groups as a powerful and well-organized people. Primarily farmers who lived in Arkansas and Missouri, they also hunted small game and the buffalo that occasionally ventured onto the tall-grass prairie.

Pawnee

The Pawnee, some 10,000, were among the largest of the farming tribes, who hunted as well. Their lands along the Platte River in Nebraska were on the border between the tall-grass prairies and the Great Plains. In origin, they were a Caddoan-speaking people who migrated from the southeast onto the Plains and north to Nebraska.

Wichita

Villagers and farmers, the Wichita were Caddoan people from the southeast who moved into Texas

▲ A Hidatsa man in a photograph taken around 1900. The Hidatsa are closely associated with the Mandan and Arikara.

and southern Kansas, living along the Arkansas River. They also went onto the high Plains to hunt buffalo. It was the Wichita that Spanish explorer Coronado encountered in 1541 as he wandered around Kansas searching for the fabled Seven Cities of Gold.

HUNTERS OF
THE GREAT PLAINS

The tribes discussed below are the major tribes of the Great Plains.

Arapaho

Originally farmers in what is now Minnesota, the Algonquian-speaking Arapaho migrated, or were pushed by other tribes, onto the Great Plains and became buffalo hunters and skilled horsemen.

They established their tepee villages in eastern Colorado and southeastern Wyoming. When buffalo appeared in their territory, the people pulled up their tepees and followed the herds.

Assiniboine

The Assiniboine were a large and powerful tribe occupying parts of Montana and the Dakotas. A Siouan-speaking people, they came originally from Canada and northern Minnesota. In winter they hunted elk and antelope to the north, and in summer raised their tepee camps on the Plains to hunt buffalo.

Blackfoot

The Algonquian-speaking Blackfoot Indians lived in northern Montana along the Canadian border. Numbering about 15,000, they included

CHILD CARE

This Sioux mother poses with her baby, who is snugly nestled in a cradleboard. The covering on the cradleboard keeps the baby warm and secure. A cradleboard could be carried on the mother's back, hung from a saddle, or carried on a travois. This photo was taken in a studio around 1900.

subtribes called the Blood and the Piegan. They carried their portable tepees with them as they hunted buffalo across the Plains.

Cheyenne

One of the most famous Plains tribes, the Cheyenne were of Algonquian origin, once living in the eastern woodlands. From there they migrated west, first to become farmers, then hunters in Wyoming. For most of the year, they roamed the Great Plains, raising their tepees in temporary camps as they tracked buffalo. The Cheyenne were superb horsemen and warriors.

Comanche

The Comanche originally lived in Wyoming. They were one of the earliest tribes to acquire the Spanish horses that had run wild and spread east and north through the Plains. From Wyoming, these skilled horsemen rode into the dry Plains of Texas and Oklahoma, at first to raid Spanish and Apache settlements for more horses. Settling in the region, they too hunted buffalo.

Crow

Relatives of the Mandan, the Crow were once farmers who migrated onto the high Plains of Montana along the Yellowstone River. As well as following the buffalo, they hunted deer, elk, and bear along the eastern slope of the Rocky Mountains. Crow men were distinguished by their long, flowing hair and the bangs they wore in front.

Kiowa

Like the Comanche, the Kiowa were expert horsemen. From Montana, they migrated south to the Red River region of Texas and Oklahoma. In summer they moved their tepees from valleys along the river to move across the Great Plains after the buffalo.

Sioux

The Sioux, also known as the Dakota, Lakota, or Nakota, were originally Woodland Indians who hunted and farmed around the Upper Mississippi, in parts of Minnesota, Wisconsin, and Iowa. Many of the farming Indians of the prairies were related to the Sioux. Pushed westward by eastern tribes, groups of the Sioux made their way to the Great Plains and became buffalo hunters and warriors. The Sioux were divided into four groups, each composed of different

▲ This young Sioux wears a feathered headdress, or bonnet. The number of feathers and how they were worn told of the wearer's achievements.

bands. The largest branch was the Teton Sioux, which numbered seven bands. The Teton, sometimes called the Western Sioux, occupied the Black Hills of South Dakota and lands in eastern Wyoming and Montana. It is the Teton Sioux, the group that migrated the farthest west, who represent, to many people, *the* Plains Indians. Great chiefs of the Teton Sioux include Sitting Bull, Red Cloud, and Crazy Horse. It was the Sioux who led the Indians to victory in the famous battle against Lieutenant Colonel George Armstrong Custer at the Little Big Horn River in Montana in 1876.

The Santee Sioux, composed of four bands, lived on the prairies, in what is now Minnesota. Although they hunted the buffalo in the prairie grasslands, they lived in permanent villages of bark-covered lodges. The Santee were more like prairie farmers than their more western relatives. The Yankton Sioux, with only one band, settled in southeastern South Dakota and in the southwest of Minnesota and Iowa. A fourth branch, the Yanktonai Sioux, with three bands, lived along the Missouri River in the eastern Dakotas. Both the Yankton and the Yanktonai farmed as well as hunted and lived in villages of earthen lodges.

THE LAND

❖ · ❖ · ❖ · ❖ · ❖ · ❖ · ❖ · ❖ · ❖ · ❖ · ❖

ANIMALS OF THE PLAINS

▲ The meat and hides of the pronghorn supplemented
buffalo products for the Plains Indians. Buckskin, made
from the hide of the antelope, was highly prized for
clothing.

▲ Buffalo, which look like huge, hump-backed, shaggy cows, belong to the cattle family. Another name for buffalo is North American bison.

◀ Prairie dogs, small animals related to squirrels, live in colonies that number in the thousands. Their underground burrows are connected and often extend for miles.

▼ A herd of buffalo grazes on the short-grass Plains. Before the arrival of white settlers, buffalo were plentiful on the Plains. Deliberate over-hunting forced the buffalo to the edge of extinction by the late 1800s. Today these animals are protected.

THE BEAUTY OF THE PLAINS

▲ Thunderclouds roll across the sky over the Black Hills of South Dakota. The name of this region comes from the dark green of its pine forests, which makes the hills seem nearly black.

▶ This landscape is typical of the dry, short-grass lands of the western Plains.

▼ The Powder River flows through the magnificent country of southeastern Montana. This land was the much-loved home of the northern Cheyenne.

❖ • ❖ • ❖ • ❖ • ❖ • ❖ • ❖ • ❖ • ❖ • ❖ • ❖

◀ The rugged Badlands in southwestern South Dakota are the result of thousands of years of erosion by wind and water. The Sioux gave the region its name ("mako sica," meaning "bad land") because it was so difficult to cross.

▼ The fantastic shapes and colors of buttes like these are typical of the landscape of the Badlands.

▲ A "sea of grass," dotted with occasional trees, once covered the eastern Plains. Here, in one of the few remaining patches of true prairie left today, flowers called dotted blazingstars poke through the tall grass.

▲ Home for many Plains Indians was a tepee, traditionally made of buffalo skins and wooden poles. The tepee is perfectly suited to a nomadic way of life. It can be taken down and put up again quickly and easily.

CHAPTER TWO

❖•❖•❖•❖•❖•❖•❖•❖•❖•❖•❖

LIVING

The prairies and the Plains contained many Indian groups. From the farmer-hunters of the prairies to the hunters of the Great Plains, their languages and ways of life were varied, although they also shared many characteristics and customs.

A nomadic way of life based on the horse and the buffalo was important to many tribes, but others led a more settled life and farmed the land at least part of the year.

PRAIRIE FARMER-HUNTERS

Dwellings

The most common architectural structure among the farmer-hunters were earth lodges, which were clustered around a central plaza or open area. The solid, round lodges were supported by rafters laid over a framework. The framework was covered first with willow branches, then a layer of grass, then some sod, and finally a layer of earth. Extending from the entrance of the lodge to the interior was a vestibule. The lodges were so solid that many people could gather on their roofs to socialize or watch ceremonies in the plaza.

The interior of the lodges were often very large. A painting of a Mandan lodge by the artist Karl Bodmer shows a family of Mandan along with their horses, dogs, and farming and hunting equipment all sharing the same space. In their ceremonial lodges, the Pawnee often dug out a shallow hole in the center of the lodge. The edge of the hole formed a kind of bench around which as many as 100 people could sit.

Inside, the hearth fire was placed in the center of the lodge below a square opening in the roof called the smoke hole. When the vestibule entrance was open, air was circulated, and the smoke from the fire drifted up through the hole.

Not all prairie dwellings were built of earth. The Osage people of Arkansas and Missouri constructed oval or rectangular lodges made of mats or skins supported by a wooden framework. An Osage lodge could be as long as 30 to 100 feet and as wide as 15 feet. The Wichita people of Kansas used grass lodges. A series of poles arranged in a circle in the ground and bent together at the top formed the framework. Other poles were attached horizontally around this foundation, which was then covered with thick grass. The Wichita homes have been described as looking like giant beehives.

The Mandan and the Arikara often built their villages on bluffs overlooking the Missouri River. From this vantage point, they could easily spot the approach of their enemies. Many villages

▲ Because the people of the prairies were basically farmers, they lived in villages of permanent homes. The most common sort of home was a rounded lodge made of earth, as shown in this photograph of Pawnee lodges in Nebraska. The family stands beneath the porchlike structure, or vestibule, at the entrance to the lodge. This photo was taken in 1873.

were also fortified. Some had earth ramparts that encircled the villages; others were protected by stockades made of wooden poles.

In addition to their permanent lodges, the farmer-hunters fashioned tepees, to be used when they went after buffalo. A typical tepee was a framework of three or four poles tied together at the top, and placed wide apart at the bottom to form a circle. Skins, usually buffalo hides, were wrapped around the framework. A flap at the top could be opened to let out smoke, and another at the bottom served as the entrance. Tepees could be put up and dismantled fairly easily as the hunters moved after the buffalo.

Growing Crops

The villages of the prairie farmers were surrounded by their fields. In the southern part of the prairies, where the growing season was longer, they raised tall corn. On the northern prairies, the Indians developed a short corn that needed less rain and a shorter growing season. The Arikara were such good farmers that they grew nine different varieties of corn. They traded their abundant crop for furs from trappers and for goods from other tribes. The Mandan also grew an abundance of corn in the fertile land

along the Missouri, and they traded with other tribes and with whites.

In addition to corn, the fields yielded squash, beans, and pumpkins. Usually there was a small plot of tobacco, which the people used in ceremonies. The women also gathered roots, wild fruits, and berries. Tending the fields was the work of the women, and the crops belonged to them. They planted, cultivated, and harvested the food. As keepers of the fields, they had authority in their villages. When a woman died, her field passed on to a daughter, sister, or other female blood relative.

The farming tools were simple digging sticks, hoes, and rakes. With the sharply pointed digging sticks, the women turned the soil and then poked holes in which they dropped the corn kernels. Corn cannot be simply scattered; it has to

▲ Homes, sometimes called lodges, were also made of reeds woven into mats and placed on a wooden frame. In a photograph taken around 1900, a family on the central Plains poses before a typical reed-mat dwelling.

be planted kernel by kernel. Hoes were fashioned from a buffalo's shoulder blade tied to a long stick. A rake could be made from a pair of deer antlers tied to a stick or a tree branch with twigs tied at the end.

Some of the harvest was eaten while it was still fresh, but most of the crop was preserved for the winter. To keep the crops, they were dried in the sun. Most of the dried corn, beans, and squash was stored in pits dug in the ground. The pits were covered with a layer of grass, on top of which were layers of skin, earth, and finally ashes. The Mandan, who were skilled potters, also stored food in pottery.

Some of the dried corn was made into cornmeal. Using a large wooden pestle, a club-shaped tool for pounding and grinding, women pounded the dried corn to a powder on rocks or in wooden bowls. It would later be mixed with meat and vegetables.

The Annual Hunt

For the prairie farmers, the buffalo hunt occurred usually once a year, in the spring or summer, when the migrating herds grazed near their territory. Leaving their fields to the care of their older people, men and women went out to gather supplies of meat and hides.

The Indians hauled their tepees, hunting gear, and the buffalo meat and hides from the hunt with a device called a travois, which was pulled by dogs. The travois was two tepee poles tied to a dog's shoulders, with the ends of the poles dragging behind. The load was placed across the poles. Later, when the Indians acquired horses, these animals pulled the travois and also carried the hunters to the buffalo. Before the horse, the hunters walked.

Once near the buffalo herd, the women set up the tepees and the men organized the hunt. Hunting was done on foot and it was a dangerous job. A wounded animal could turn on a hunter, who was armed only with a stone-tipped lance or bow and arrows, and trample him to death.

Hunting techniques varied, but one effective method was to stampede the herd. By setting fire to the grass, hunters would drive them off a cliff. Sometimes the hunters stampeded the buffalo past groups of men who then attacked them with a shower of arrows.

Once the kills were made, the favorite parts of the animals, the tongue and liver, were eaten on the spot. Since fresh meat would not last on the journey back to the village, it had to be preserved as quickly as possible. This was the job of the women. The women cut the large chunks of meat into strips and dried them on racks in the sun or over slow-burning fires. Some of the dried meat was pounded with stones into a powder, which was then mixed with buffalo fat and berries. The resulting mixture, called pemmican, lasted for months. While some women prepared the meat, others stretched the hides on stakes in the ground and scraped them. Later in the village, the hides would be made into robes and covers for the tepees. At the end of the hunt, whatever meat and hides could be dragged by the dogs or carried on the backs of the women was taken back to the village.

With the arrival of the horse, hunting became quicker and easier. The hunt lasted longer, and more meat and hides could be gathered and carried. Although the prairie Indians came to depend more and more on the buffalo, they still remained farmers. They did not give up their lands until they were forced out by settlers.

Clothing on the Prairie

Prairie farmers clothed themselves in buckskins. Men wore shirts and leggings made of deer and elk skin, and their robes were generally of buffalo hide. Their moccasins were fashioned from deer

▲ Before the Indians obtained horses from the earliest European explorers, dogs were used to haul travois. Even after the Indians acquired horses, they still used dogs to carry lighter loads.

or buffalo skin. Pawnee and Osage men wore buckskin breechcloths, or aprons, secured around the waist. Women generally wore one-piece buckskin dresses.

Prairie people liked to decorate their clothing with porcupine quills, elk teeth, shells, and glass beads and pieces of metal obtained from traders. Sometimes, they painted their clothes, especially their robes, with animals or scenes depicting their exploits as hunters. They were very talented in shaping beautiful and intricate geometric designs. Many paintings and drawings of the Indians show them in their most elaborate ceremonial regalia. Everyday outfits were simpler.

Headdresses and hairstyles of the people were also elaborate and varied. Pawnee and Osage men shaved their heads except for a strip in the middle. To the strip they attached a brush of deer-tail hairs, called a roach. They usually dyed the roach red and might add feathers. Kansa men plucked all the hair from their heads except for a small lock at the back. Arikara men wore their hair long, but with a front knot or crest of hair

swept up and held in place by pieces of bone. (The name Arikara means "horns," which these pieces of bone resembled as they stuck up from a man's head.) Mandan men also wore their hair long, sometimes with a short braid at the side, or sometimes with the side hair cut shorter.

The kind and position of the feathers that the men wore in their hair signified their achievements as either a hunter or a warrior. The arrangement of the feathers varied to suit the meaning; they might hang down in the hair, or they might stand up, or be thrust through a clump of hair.

The feathered headdresses or bonnets people think of as typical were for special occasions or to denote a person's status. Many of them were war bonnets. Made of eagle feathers attached to a

▲ The magnificent ceremonial regalia of this Mandan chief was worn only on special occasions. His trailing war bonnet is topped by buffalo horns decorated with ermine tails. Only a chief of great renown wore buffalo horns.

leather band, they were often so long that they streamed down the wearer's back to reach the ground. The longer the tail of feathers, the greater the wearer's exploits.

Necklaces were also a favorite kind of adornment. Some were bear or wolf claws or animal bones and teeth strung together. Others might be made of pieces of metal or glass beads. Many Indians wore ear decorations as well. These too might be made of beads or metal or bone.

Part of the Indians' decoration was painting their bodies. They used dyes from plants and from colored clay mixed with water. They wore paint in warfare and in special ceremonies. Mandan chiefs also tattooed their bodies.

Families on the Prairie

Prairie farmers lived in extended families. Parents, children, grandparents, aunts, and uncles might all share the same lodge. Families were also part of a larger system of clans. Clan members, even if they lived in different lodges, claimed descent from the same ancestor. In fact, people in several different villages might be members of the same clan. They were all considered relatives.

In some prairie tribes, clan heritage was traced through women; in others it was traced through men. Depending on this, children belonged either to their mother's clan or their father's clan. In some tribes, members of the same clan could not intermarry; in others, members could only marry within their clans.

Women were in charge of the fields; they were also in charge of the household, and thus they made the tools and utensils. They sewed the family's clothing and built the tepees, as well as decorating them, often with beautiful geometric designs. They were very skilled at making beadwork, which was used to decorate necklaces, armbands, earrings, headbands, and clothing.

Children too were cared for by the women. Infants were tucked into stiff-backed cradleboards made of sticks and covered with soft skins to make a sacklike container. Mothers carried the babies on their backs as they worked. A cradleboard could also be carried on a travois, on horseback, or propped against a tepee or a pole inside a lodge.

The men were the hunters and the warriors. They made the bows and the arrows and lances, stone-tipped at first and later made with metal, used in hunting and warfare. They also tended to the horses. Part of their work was to educate boys and young men in the skills of hunting and warfare. And they governed the tribe, holding councils and making decisions about hunting and warfare. Some men became shamans, or medicine men. Shamans foretold the future and practiced curing—diagnosing illness and treating the sick with prayers and herbs.

The children were taught the skills that would help their tribe survive. By the time they were 10 years old, girls had learned to tend the crops, cook, fashion clothing, and practice all the other skills of the older women. Boys followed in their fathers' footsteps. They learned to ride, hunt, and make weapons. They practiced their marksmanship in competitions with one another. By the

▲ A bear claw necklace, such as this Oto man wears, was an ornament and also a mark of bravery, for it told that the hunter had risked his life to kill the ferocious animal.

▲ Two Indian babies peek from their decorated cradle-boards. The hoods kept the sun and rain off the babies. Infants in cradleboards could easily be carried on their mothers' backs.

time boys were 13, they often went on hunts to sharpen their skills.

Warfare

Generally people think of the Indians of the Great Plains as the most fearsome of the western warriors. Much of their reputation for fierceness comes from the fact that they fought desperately to save their lands from the settlers, traders, and hunters who continuously pushed westward.

However, prairie tribes also went to war, mostly against one another. One tribe might be after the same herd of buffalo as another, thus causing a dispute over hunting grounds. Or since horses were so highly prized, tribes might raid one another for these valued animals. In lean times, tribes also raided one another for food. Other tribes fought because of old hostilities between them. The Santee Sioux, for instance, were traditional enemies of the Chippewa of northern Minnesota because the Chippewa, when they acquired guns from traders in the 1600s, drove the Sioux from the woodlands.

Whatever the reason, the warfare itself was less important than the courage shown by the warriors. A warrior's greatest victory was simply to touch an enemy with his bare hands while the enemy was armed and surrounded by his own men. This was not an easy feat, and warriors who accomplished this were considered the bravest. Among the prairie farmers, warfare was a sport, not just battles to be won.

Warriors prepared themselves for a war party by dancing. The purpose was to acquire power and courage. The motions of the dance dramatized the moves of warfare: chasing the enemy, leaping toward him, striking a blow with the hand. After the battle, warriors also danced to celebrate. Dances were accompanied by songs and drumbeats.

Boasting of one's deeds was also part of warfare. But the exploits recounted in front of the other warriors had to be accurate, for the others had kept careful watch and knew what had occurred. Anyone who lied was shamed as listeners jeered and hooted.

HUNTERS OF THE GREAT PLAINS

Between the fertile prairies of the eastern Plains and the Rocky Mountins of the West lay the seemingly endless open spaces of the Great Plains. With scant and uncertain rainfall, often dry river beds, and tough sod, or soil, the area was not suited for farming. The Indians depended almost completely on the buffalo for their food, clothing, and shelter.

Origins of the Hunters

Evidence indicates that prehistoric hunters existed thousands of years ago on the Great Plains. It is not certain what happened to these hunters. There is some evidence that later farming villages existed along the river beds of the Great Plains. It is thought by some archaeologists that these farmers, who also made pottery, were connected to the early farming culture of the Ohio Valley. By the time Europeans arrived, the people of the Great Plains were once again hunters.

Historians conclude that the oldest of the Great Plains tribes is the Blackfoot, although they do not know exactly when they appeared in the area. They do believe, however, that the Blackfoot migrated south from Canada and then spread out into most of what is now Montana. The Blackfoot were actually a confederacy of three tribes—the others being the Blood and the Piegan—who spoke the same language and shared a common Algonquian origin.

It is also thought that the Crow people appeared on the Great Plains several centuries ago. They broke off from their relatives, the Siouan-speaking Mandan, and abandoned their farms and villages along the Missouri River to become buffalo hunters in southern Montana.

Then, in the 1700s, there began a mass movement of people onto the Great Plains. The Cree and Assiniboine moved from the forests of Canada and northern Minnesota to the prairies and then onto the Great Plains. From the eastern prairies around the upper Mississippi came the Cheyenne, the Arapaho, and the Sioux. From near the Rockies in western Wyoming and Montana, the Comanche and Kiowa moved onto the central and southern Great Plains.

This eruption of people onto the Great Plains did not happen overnight. At the same time, it was a very short process compared to the millennia that had passed since the arrival of the first Americans. In about 200 years, from the beginning of the 18th century to the end of the 19th,

▲ The word "tepee" comes from a Sioux word meaning "the place where a person lives." Warm in the winter and cool in the summer, tepees were large enough to house an entire family and its household goods comfortably.

the culture of the Great Plains people took root, flourished, and vanished.

From the east the Sioux, Assiniboine, Arapaho, and Cheyenne were steadily driven onto the Great Plains by their Indian enemies who had obtained the white man's guns. From the west came the Comanche and Kiowa, who rode onto the Plains on their newly acquired horses. In a short time the tribes driven from the east changed from farmers into buffalo hunters, creating a Plains culture centered around the horse.

Horses originated in North America, from where, in prehistoric times, they wandered into Asia, Europe, and Africa. However, by the end of the Ice Age, they had become extinct in the New World. Not until the 1500s were they reintro-

duced. In 1519, the Spanish conquistador Hernán Cortés landed on the east coast of Mexico. With him were 10 stallions, five mares, and a foal. From this beginning, hundreds of thousands of horses spread throughout North America, establishing themselves on their native continent.

When the Spanish pushed from Mexico into the Southwest and California, herds of horses accompanied them. Indians of the Southwest stole hundreds in raids and then traded them to tribes in the mountains of the Northwest. Further herds escaped and ran wild on the northern Plains. By the early 1700s, the tribes of the Great Plains had become a horse culture.

Horses changed the lives of the Plains people. Before, as were the farmer-hunters of the prairies, Plains Indians were limited in what they could kill and transport. But, unlike the prairie Indians, the hunters of the Plains had no crops to fall back on. Now, they could expand their hunting grounds, going after herds for miles and miles. Hunters could chase down more herds and easily surround them. More buffalo products could be taken and carried off. Meat, hides, fat, and bones were plentiful. And a horse, unlike a dog, could drag a dozen or more 30-foot tepee poles. More and longer poles meant a tepee could be covered with as many as 20 hides, creating a much larger home. Because of horses, there was more food, better dwellings, more clothing, more products to trade, leisure time for ceremonies, and more time for war.

Great Plains Dwellings

The permanent, as well as mobile, homes of the Great Plains' hunters were tepees. They were similar in construction to those of the prairie Indians but were larger and more spacious. The poles of the frame often extended four or five feet above the buffalo-hide covering. Generally, the basic frame was three sturdy poles set in the ground and tied at the top. More poles (as many as 16) were then leaned against this frame. Buffalo hides, tanned into leather, were sewn together and stretched over the framework. Two long poles on either side held open the flap at the top, and another flap opened at the bottom. A tepee village was arranged in a circle, partly for protection from enemies and partly for the gatherings at ceremonies and councils held in the center of the village.

HUNTING BUFFALO

Artist George Catlin sketched this scene of a buffalo hunt in 1844. Hunting buffalo with spears and bows and arrows was dangerous. A hunter could be injured or even killed if he fell from his horse or was charged by a wounded animal. The thong trailing from the horse of the hunter on the right was used if the rider fell. He would grab the thong to try to slow down or stop his horse so he could remount.

▲ An Indian woman scrapes a buffalo hide she has staked on the ground. This is one step in the long, laborious process of turning the hide into leather.

The women constructed the tepees, but the men decorated them, and usually very elaborately. Pictures of animals, geometric designs, and symbols were painted on the skins. Many of the designs reflected the bravery or deeds of the owner as a hunter or warrior. Others identified a family. Among the Kiowa, it was common for tepee designs, which became a kind of coat of arms, to be passed from one generation to another. No other family could use that design.

Buffalo Hunting

The horse, and later the guns and tools obtained from traders, created the Great Plains way of life—which was hunting and warfare. Moving their camps from place to place, the Indians pursued the herds during the spring and summer and into the autumn. The winter could be a lean time, when the herds moved south. Often, a tribe would divide into small groups in the winter,

each hunting whatever game it could find.

When spring came, the tribe gathered again and the annual hunt began. Sometimes two or three tribes hunted together. An encampment might include more than 1,000 tepees arranged in a huge circle.

Hunting was a highly disciplined ritual. Certain men of the tribe, selected because of their bravery and skill, acted as "police." They organized the hunters into groups and made sure that the men acted together. No hunter was allowed to rush out on his own and perhaps scare off the herd. If anyone disobeyed this rule, his weapons and hunting gear and even his tepee might be burned to the ground.

▲ These moccasins were worn by a Comanche in the late 19th century. They are made of buckskin that has been painted, beaded, and fringed; the metal tips are called jingles because of the sound they make as the wearer walks.

The strategy of the hunt was to surround a herd and try to cause the animals to mill around in confusion. Then the hunters closed in on the herd, their highly trained "buffalo" horses galloping as close as possible to a buffalo so the hunter could shoot accurately and swiftly. When one buffalo was downed, a hunter chased another and another until his arrows were used up. When the hunt was over, each hunter kept the animals he had killed. Since each hunter had his own specially marked arrows, he could instantly identify his buffalo.

A successful hunt meant fresh meat for the whole camp and was a time to celebrate with singing and dancing. It was also the time for the women to prepare the meat and work on the buffalo hides. They preserved meat in the same way as the prairie farmers, by drying strips on racks over a fire. Some of the dried meat was pounded into pemmican, which was then stored for the winter in sacks called parfleches.

Plains women were highly skilled in tanning, or making a hide into leather. Immediately after a buffalo was killed, the women skinned it and stretched the hide on the ground with stakes. They rubbed a mixture of buffalo brains and liver into both sides of the hide and then rolled up the skin and let it stand overnight for the mixture to soak in.

After this the hide was washed and dried. Since it would shrink and harden, it had to be pulled back into shape. The next step was graining, which was done by first rubbing the hide with a rough stone and then pulling it back and forth through a loop of rope. The hide was soaked again and staked out on the ground. The inside was scraped with a knife, and the hide was then bleached for two days in the sun. This step was repeated, this time on the hair side. If the hair didn't come off too easily, the hide was soaked in a mixture of ashes and water. For two days, the hide again bleached in the sun—and was finally ready to be made into a robe or a tepee covering.

Nearly every part of the buffalo was used in some way. The hides were fashioned into clothing and tepees, tough leather shields, drums, and rawhide thongs. Bones were carved into tools and ornaments. Horns served as spoons and other utensils and stomachs were cleaned to become cooking pots. Ceremonial rattles were made from hoofs, which were also cooked to make glue. Winter boots were stuffed with buffalo hair for warmth. Balls for games and decorative ornaments were also made from hair. And because wood was scarce, buffalo dung, or "chips," fueled the fires.

Clothing

The dress of the Indians of the Great Plains was like that of the prairie farmers. Men wore buckskin leggings and shirts, often heavily fringed, and robes and moccasins of buffalo hide. Women dressed in simple, one-piece shifts. And like the prairie farmers, they added elaborate decorations to their best finery.

Porcupine quills, elk teeth, beads, buffalo hair, and pieces of glass and metal were all used and crafted into beautiful embroidery work by the women. The men often painted their clothing, especially their buffalo robes, as well as their shields. The paintings on a robe might tell a story of a warrior's daring in battle or his power as a hunter. Sometimes a robe served simply as a record of daily events. Important events in a tribe's history were also recorded on a buffalo robe. These robes were called winter counts. The robe was the tribe's calendar, each year marked by a significant event such as a victory in battle or a good hunt.

The way in which the Plains warriors decorated themselves told of their rank and their accomplishments. Among the Crow Indians, it was the custom for the successful chief of a war party to attach hair to his shirt and moccasins. If a Crow warrior was able to take a weapon from an enemy, he was entitled to wear ermine skins on his shirt.

Feathers were particularly important as an indication of a man's achievements in warfare. How they were marked showed how an enemy was overcome. A split feather said the warrior had wounded his enemy many times. The death of an enemy was signified by a hole in the quill, or stem, of a feather.

Plains Indians wore their hair long, sometimes parting it into two braids and sometimes free flowing. Crow men were particularly distin-

▲ A Cheyenne/Arapaho war shirt from the late 19th century. Made of buckskin, the shirt is decorated with painting, beadwork, and fringes.

guished by their long hair, which often reached well below their waist. The painter George Catlin, who traveled among the Plains Indians in the early 1800s, commented on the hair of one Crow chief. The chief, appropriately called Long Hair, bound his hair in a leather strap from his head to the hair's end. Catlin noted that the chief then folded the hair into a package that he carried under his arm. On special occasions he unwrapped the package, oiled his hair with bear grease, and spread it upon the ground. Crow men wore the front of their hair in bangs. For warfare, they stiffened the bangs with bear grease—they stood straight up from their foreheads.

Headdresses too were highly ornamented, although most were for ceremonial purposes. The headdress (often called a bonnet) of a Blackfoot medicine society member was decorated with buffalo horns and ermine tails. A Blackfoot chief in his full regalia often wore a headdress whose feathers stood straight up from his head. Necklaces of bone, teeth, claws, metal, and beads were also common.

Plains Indians decorated, not only their tepees and their clothing, but just about everything that

▲ Sioux men did not shave their heads. They grew their hair long and often attached a sort of topknot, called a roach, to it. This portrait of a Sioux man was taken in 1899.

could be decorated. Their weapons of war—shields and lances—were painted or trimmed with feathers, fur, fringe, and sometimes the scalps of enemies. Tobacco pouches, parfleches, baby carriers, pipe bags, knife sheaths, and ceremonial objects such as rattles were all adorned with porcupine quills, fringe, or beadwork.

Great Plains Families

The structure of the Plains Indians family was similar to that of the prairie farmers. Most tribes had a system of clans, some of which traced their descent through the mother and others of which traced lineage through the father. If descent was through the mother, a husband lived in his wife's village; if through the father, the wife moved to her husband's camp.

Marriage was a formal matter, but it was not arranged by parents or relatives. If a young man was interested in a young woman, he courted her. He might try to win her favor by showing off his skills of horsemanship, standing upright or slipping under the belly of his galloping pony. Sometimes he would appear at her tepee to entertain her by playing music on a flute.

Among the Cheyenne, courtship was a long process. Cheyenne women were noted for their purity and proper behavior, and there were strict rules about courting. It might take as long as four years for a man to finally win the bride of his choice. He would follow her around as she did her tasks, trying to get her attention by calling or whistling after her. Before they could even meet outside her tepee, she would have to have several conversations with him. Once she consented to marry him, the families were consulted and the wedding took place. If the young woman did not like the man, all his courtship was in vain, for she would never speak to him.

When the formal ceremony took place, the groom presented the bride's parents with as many of the finest horses he could obtain. Horses were a young man's bank account, the measure of his wealth. The more horses a young man presented, the higher he was esteemed by his bride and her family. The prestige of the young woman and her family was also enhanced.

Polygamy, the practice of a man having more than one wife, was not uncommon. However, it usually occurred among warriors or chiefs, whose influence and wealth in the clan were prominent. Polygamy, for instance, was allowed among the Sioux. The painter George Catlin visited frequently with the son of a prominent

▲ This young Cheyenne woman exhibits the modest demeanor expected of her. Cheyenne women were noted for their modesty and virtue.

Sioux chief who had four young wives. Catlin noted that they all shared the same large tepee and seemed to live in harmony. He also observed that among the Sioux, there were three times as many women as men, so the arrangement was a practical one. The women were protected and provided for, more children would be born into the family, and the work and skills of the women brought honor and prestige to the family and clan.

When they were not hunting or warring, the men gathered to discuss the affairs of the village: perhaps an upcoming ceremony, a dispute between families, the next raiding party to gather horses. They made and repaired weapons, taught men's skills to the boys, and played games.

As well as accompanying men on the hunt, the women did the work of the village. They made the dwellings and clothing, cooked the food, gathered plants, and cared for the children.

▲ In this photo, a Sioux boy wears a feathered head-dress, beaded shirt, and beaded sash. His clothing was probably borrowed from his father just for this picture, taken around 1900.

In some tribes, such as the Sioux, women became healers, using herbs, poultices, chants, and even hypnosis. Often, older women were called on to give advice about religion and rituals and to counsel others.

Children were eagerly anticipated and from early infancy were taught probably the most important rule of the tribe; no one could endanger the people by unnecessary cries or noise that would alert an enemy or frighten off a herd of buffalo. Beyond that, children were seldom punished but they were not coddled either. It was considered that restraints or restrictions would rob them of their spirit of independence.

Until they were about seven or eight, boys and girls stayed fairly close to their mothers. Like other children, they played games and were given toys. Their playthings reflected the roles they would play when they grew up—dolls and little tepees for the girls and small bows, arrows, shields, and lances for the boys. Both boys and girls also played with animal dolls—buffalo, bear, and elk.

As they grew older, children began learning the skills of their parents. Both boys and girls became expert riders. Indian horses had no saddles and the bridles were a piece of rope looped around a horse's lower jaw. Children learned to guide their swift ponies by the pressure of their knees and legs, just as the adults did.

Shooting at targets, racing their ponies, watching the men make the hunting gear and weapons were all practice for the time when a boy would join the hunt or a war party. Boys also joined together to listen to the older men recount the history of the tribe and explain the important ideas and beliefs of the people.

Girls did not join in the activities of the boys. They prepared for marriage and the work of the women. They helped carry water and gather buffalo chips for the fires. They learned to tan hides and build tepees and sew clothing. They dried meat and made pemmican. One of their most important skills was to create the unique embroidery work on clothes, moccasins, and ornaments. However, girls and young women were taught to shoot a small bow and how to use a knife. It was important for them to know how to defend themselves against an enemy.

Warfare

Hunting was the major occupation of the Indians of the Plains; but warfare too was an important element of their way of life. It was not warfare as many people think of it, with large armies marching to meet each other and then doing battle. Plains war was a series of swift raids by one group against another. The basic idea was to gain honor and glory by avenging an attack or better yet, by capturing as many horses as possible. Taking horses was a major objective of raids, not because a tribe necessarily needed them, but because the possession of horses was a sure sign of success—and prestige.

Raids were carried out by bands of warriors, often following an individual man who was seeking personal honors. The band would sneak up on an enemy camp and try to make off with as many horses as it could. It was especially honorable to steal the favorite horses of an important chief, who usually kept his mounts right by his tepee.

If the raiders were discovered, the camp natu-

▲ Eagle feathers adorn the round shield of this Sioux man. He holds a bow and several arrows in his right hand.

▲ When Native American groups were displaced from their territory, by other tribes or by white settlers, they trespassed on the land of other groups, causing conflict. Before white explorers and settlers brought firearms, Indians fought with a variety of weapons, including lances, war clubs, and bows and arrows. They defended themselves with round shields of hardened buffalo hide. Weapons were often elaborately decorated, as shown by the lances and shield carried by this Sioux man.

rally resisted and tried to fight off the attackers. But more important than killing an enemy was delivering a blow to his body with a weapon or even with the bare hands. This was called making a coup. (Pronounced *coo*, the word is French for a "blow.") Shooting an enemy with an arrow or a gun from a distance did not count among the Indians as making coup.

Plains Indians did take the scalps of their enemies if they had time during a raid. However, except for the Sioux and the Cree, the scalps of enemies were not considered an important trophy. Regarding scalping, many historians believe that the practice was not widespread until the coming of whites, who gave bounties for Indian scalps. In addition, the stereotype of the Plains Indian as a grisly torturer of captives is not valid. Experts believe that torture of captives was not a tradition among the people of the Plains. Few authentic records exist of any such widespread torture as depicted in western stories. Leading a successful raiding party, counting coups on many enemies, and taking many horses brought honors to a warrior. But this did not necessarily mean that the man was a chief or had authority in governing the tribe, although he would certainly be respected and his opinions listened to.

Although warfare among the tribes had the aspect of sport, it was nevertheless deadly. Raids of one tribe upon another brought counterattacks for revenge. Some tribes became bitter enemies, seemingly in constant warfare. Territorial disputes were one cause, as a tribe tried to move into another's territory. The Sioux fought the Shoshone, who came onto the Plains from the mountains. Around the Arkansas River in the southern Plains, the southern Cheyenne fought the Comanche and the Kiowa.

LIVING ON THE LAND

❖ • ❖ • ❖ • ❖ • ❖ • ❖ • ❖ • ❖ • ❖

PLANTS OF IMPORTANCE

◀ Corn seeds must be deliberately planted, but then the plants require little attention until they are ready to be harvested. Plains Indians often planted their corn crop before they left to follow the buffalo; when they returned weeks later, the corn was ripe.

▼ Indian farmers of the Plains planted squash and bean seeds along with their corn seeds. As the corn stalks grew, they formed supports for the squash and bean plants.

❖ • ❖ • ❖ • ❖ • ❖ • ❖ • ❖ • ❖ • ❖ • ❖

HOMES

▶ A tepee village is one of the sights at the annual Crow Festival held near the Custer battlefield site in Montana. Tepees today are made from canvas, not buffalo hides.

▼ These earth lodges at Fort Lincoln State Park in North Dakota are accurate replicas of Mandan homes.

HORSES

▲ The Absaroka Mountains of western Montana are the background for these grazing horses. The introduction of the horse changed the life of the Plains Indians.

▲ Mustangs run wild in Theodore Roosevelt National Park in North Dakota. These horses are descendants of the original Spanish herds that spread northward from Mexico starting in the mid-1500s.

EVERYDAY LIFE

◄ This deerskin dress was worn by a Cheyenne woman. It is decorated with fringes and colorful beadwork.

▶ Because the people of the Plains followed the buffalo at least part of every year, they needed containers that were light and unbreakable. This storage bag, or parfleche, is made of painted leather.

▼ This beautifully painted buffalo robe was worn by a Cheyenne child.

▲ Wearing a beautifully feathered costume, this man carries a feathered ceremonial lance. The lance and the buffalo skull were part of a ceremony meant to bring the buffalo to the hunters.

CHAPTER THREE

RITUALS AND RELIGION

The beliefs, customs, and rituals of the people of the prairies and the Great Plains were similar. As discussed earlier, most of the tribes of the Great Plains came from the east. Although they adopted the lives of hunters, they still retained ideas and customs from their original homelands. For instance, both the farming Mandan and the hunting Sioux carried out the ritual of the Sun Dance. In fact, most prairie and Plains tribes shared this ceremony.

Both groups also shared the basic belief in nature as the all-powerful spirit. For the Indians, the spirits lived in the sun, rain, wind, the earth, and in animals and plants. Their rituals and ceremonies were directed toward this force, which guided nearly every aspect of their lives. Whites generally referred to this force as the Great Spirit.

Among the tribes the spirit was given different names. The Blackfoot called the spirit Napi, the old man, and they believed he created the world and everything in it. For the Sioux, the spirit was Wakan Tanka, who sent them the animals of the Plains for their food.

According to Assiniboine beliefs, Wakan Tanka gave each person four souls. Three of the souls died when the body died. The fourth soul remained alive as a spirit bundle and would finally be released to Wakan Tanka after friends of the dead person brought gifts.

Among the Kiowa, the chief spirit was the sun. The Pawnee's great spirit was Tirarwa, who, along with the sun and the stars, guided the lives of the people.

Religious ceremonies were generally conducted by a medicine man, or shaman, who was believed to have special healing and spiritual powers, obtained through visions. But it was not just shamans who sought and received visions, but all the men of the tribe if they wished to be great hunters and warriors.

VISIONS

One of the most important religious concepts among the Indians was that of the quest for a vision. Seeking and receiving a vision would protect and guide a warrior through his entire life. Usually when he was about 15, a young man set out to find his own particular vision. In order to do so, he had to be alone. Separating himself from the tribe, the young man fasted, prayed, and very often tortured himself in some way. Through these sacrifices, he experienced a vision through which he found his special spirit with

whom he would communicate. The spirit might be an animal, the wind, a bird—always some part of nature.

The spirit told the young man which sacred objects to put together in a medicine bundle, the objects that would bring success in war and hunting, sometimes healing powers, and long life. A medicine bundle might contain corn, animal bones, tobacco or sage, and a special stone or stick. Throughout his life, a man sought guidance from his special spirit, which was embodied in his medicine bundle.

Among most tribes, it was common for a young man who wanted special sacred powers to spend time in a sweat lodge to purify himself. Inside the sweat lodge, which was a simple wood-frame hut covered by buffalo skins, the young man sat with older men who would guide him. They built a fire, and as they chanted prayers, rubbed themselves with sage to purify their bodies. They were allowed to drink water but not to spill any. Water was precious and wasting it would anger the spirit of thunder, who might later severely test the young man and try to make

THE VISION QUEST

Dreams and visions were important to all Native Americans as a way to come into contact with the spirit world. This contact gave power, or "medicine," to those who sought it. Among the tribes of the Plains, an attempt to have a vision was called a vision quest. Those facing important moments such as an approaching battle sought visions in various ways.

Going on a vision quest usually began with a ritual sweatbath. The seeker then went off by himself to an isolated place and fasted, often for days at a time. Some Plains tribes also used peyote, a hallucinogenic drug, to induce visions, but this was not a widespread practice until after 1890.

If a seeker experienced a vision, he would then talk with a medicine man to discover its meaning. After the vision was understood, a personal medicine bundle was prepared. A person's medicine bundle was made of objects related to his vision. For example, if a warrior had a vision of an eagle and then found an eagle feather soon after, he would add the feather to his medicine bundle. The bundle was wrapped in hide or put into a small pouch. Individual medicine bundles were usually worn around the neck or attached to a shield.

The sacred pipes belonging to the whole tribe were kept in medicine bundles, along with other objects of significance to the tribe. The tribe's medicine bundle was the special responsibility of the chief or medicine man.

▲ Among the Plains Indians, medicine men like this
Crow leader were revered for their spiritual powers. The
coiled knot of his hair signifies his role.

▲ This Hidatsa man carries an elaborately decorated calumet, or pipe. The bowl of a true calumet was carved from a type of soft stone now called catlinite after the famous artist George Catlin.

pecially if the other person was favored with a variety or many visions. The receiver learned the songs and prayers and was allowed to copy the medicine bundle of the more fortunate warrior.

TRADITIONAL STORIES

The traditional stories of the Plains people reached far back in time. Through their stories, and the ceremonies that surrounded them, they remembered their heritage and kept it alive.

Among the Mandan, the origins of humankind on earth are explained by a creation story. Long, long ago, the people lived underground, in a village near a large lake. A gigantic vine grew up through to the earth above. Some Mandan climbed up the vine to the upper world, and found that it was sunny and full of animals to hunt and food to gather. They returned to the underground village and persuaded everyone to climb the vine to the surface above.

An important tale of the Sioux tells how they obtained the calumet. In ancient times, a beautiful young woman approached a Sioux camp carrying a pipe. She gave it to a chief and told him that it was sacred. All who smoked the pipe together would live in peace. As the young woman left the camp, she suddenly turned into a buffalo calf, and then, before the astonished eyes of the people, lay on the ground and arose as a white buffalo. Albino animals appeared from time to time, but because they were unusual, the Indians looked upon them with awe and respect. From that time on, the White Buffalo Maiden and the calumet were especially revered by the Sioux.

According to the Cheyenne, they exist as a people because of their legendary hero, Sweet Medicine. Early in Cheyenne history, Sweet Medicine traveled to the sacred mountains in the Black Hills of the Dakotas. There the great spirit, Maiyun, gave him four sacred arrows. Two were for war, which gave the people power over their enemies, and two were for hunting, so the people would never go hungry. The sacred arrows were kept in a special medicine bundle, and once a year, the Cheyenne gathered in a ceremony to renew the arrows.

The Kiowa revered a place called Devil's Tower in eastern Wyoming, the region from which they originally came. The legend says that in ancient times, a brother and his seven sisters were playing when suddenly the boy turned into a ferocious bear. The bear chased the sisters to a tree stump, which spoke, telling them to climb as

▲ This drawing from around 1884 shows a Comanche chief in full ceremonial dress. He holds two calumets, or sacred tobacco pipes.

him afraid. A young man who was afraid would not be able to experience a vision. When the young man completed the ritual in the sweat lodge, he then went out alone to find his vision.

A young man might receive more than one vision. If so, this meant he was capable of receiving special prayers and dreams. In such a case, the man was destined to become a shaman who would guide religious ceremonies and practice spiritual healing.

Often, to help him gain added power, a seeker after visions carried with him the calumet, or sacred pipe. The calumet was an object of special reverence, which was used in dances and rituals and was also a symbol of peace. When tribes smoked the calumet together, they signified their intention to live in peace.

Not everyone received a vision, and it was not considered a disgrace to fail. The unsuccessful seeker could buy the use of another's dreams, es-

LEGENDS

The different tribes of the Plains tell many stories about the creation of the earth, its peoples, and their culture. The tales of one group are often slightly different from the tales of another.

THE ORIGIN OF THE SIOUX

❖ · ❖ · ❖ · ❖ · ❖ · ❖ · ❖ · ❖ · ❖ · ❖

When the world was young, a water monster caused a great flood. To escape the rising water, a young woman climbed a high hill. A great eagle swooped down to rescue her and carried her off to his nest on the top of the tallest mountain. Soon the nest was the only place in the whole world not covered with water, and the woman was the only human being alive. She stayed with the eagle, and soon she had twin children, a girl and a boy. When the water finally sank again, the eagle brought the woman and her children back to their land. The eagle, the young woman, and the twin children are the ancestors of all the Sioux.

THE ORIGIN OF THE CHEYENNE SUN DANCE

❖ · ❖ · ❖ · ❖ · ❖ · ❖ · ❖ · ❖ · ❖ · ❖

Long, long ago there was a terrible drought. The plants and animals died, and the Cheyenne people had nothing to eat. Then a medicine man had a vision telling him to travel with his wife far to the north, to the sacred medicine lodge of Maheo, the creator. They traveled for many days and finally reached a huge mountain. A passage led them into the mountain to Maheo's medicine lodge. There Maheo taught them the proper way to perform the sacred Sun Dance. He told them that if the Cheyenne performed the Sun Dance correctly every year, they would have many buffalo and never be hungry again. The medicine man and his wife returned to their people and taught them the dance—and after that the Cheyenne always performed the Sun Dance correctly and always had buffalo.

HOW THE BLACKFOOT GOT TOBACCO

❖ • ❖ • ❖ • ❖ • ❖ • ❖ • ❖ • ❖ • ❖ • ❖ • ❖

The first Blackfoot people to learn about the sacred tobacco were four brothers. A spirit told them how to grow the plant and how to make pipes. The spirit explained that if the Blackfoot people smoked tobacco with the proper ceremonies, the smoke would carry their prayers up to the Great Spirit and they would have peace and happiness. Finally, the spirit told the brothers to teach the rest of the tribe about tobacco. But the brothers decided not to share the secret of tobacco. They planted the seeds in a hidden place and formed a Tobacco Society of just the four of them. Instead of peace and happiness, the Blackfoot had war and anger.

A young man named Bull-by-Himself decided to go look for tobacco, since the four brothers wouldn't give the people any. He searched and searched, but he couldn't find the plant growing anywhere. Just as he was about to give up, he came upon some beavers. As soon as they saw him, the beavers changed into handsome men. They told him all about the proper ways to use tobacco and gave him some seeds. Bull-by-Himself went home and showed the Blackfoot how to plant the seeds. Their plants grew well, but the secret tobacco patch of the four brothers was destroyed by a hailstorm. Ever since then, the Blackfoot have used tobacco to honor the Great Spirit and bring peace to the people.

THE SIOUX STORY OF BEAR MOUNTAIN

❖ • ❖ • ❖ • ❖ • ❖ • ❖ • ❖ • ❖ • ❖ • ❖

Once two Sioux boys wandered away from the camp and got lost. For several days they tried to find their way home, but they got even more lost instead. Then they saw a giant grizzly bear—and the bear saw them. The boys began to run away and pray to Wakan Tanka for help. Wakan Tanka heard their cries. Suddenly the earth they were on began to rise up from the ground, carrying the boys with it. Finally, when the earth had risen more than a thousand feet into the air, it stopped and became solid rock. The giant grizzly bear was so angry that he clawed deep scratches into the rock, but he couldn't reach the boys. He went away, and Wakan Tanka sent a huge eagle to carry the boys down from the rock. Ever since then, this place has been important to the Sioux, who sometimes call it Bear Mountain. Today it is better known as Devil's Tower, a name given to it by white settlers who had little respect for Indian beliefs.

▲ In the painting shown here, dating from 1874, the Sioux hold their traditional Sun Dance.

high as they could. As the girls frantically climbed upward, the stump rose into the sky, carrying them with it. The seven sisters remained in the sky as the stars of the Big Dipper. The place where they ascended is called Devil's Tower, and the Kiowa believe the seven sisters watch over and protect their earth-dwelling brothers and sisters.

THE SUN DANCE

For both the prairie farmers and the Plains hunters, one of the most important ceremonies was the Sun Dance. The name *Sun Dance*, however, is not quite accurate, since the ritual was not designed to worship the sun but to bring powerful visions to the participants as well as to renew the people and the earth, to give thanks to the spirits, to protect the people from danger or illness, to fulfill a vow, or to pray for increased fertility.

Generally, the Sun Dance occurred yearly, and great preparations were made. The men cut down a large tree that would be made into a tall pole and set up in the center of a specially constructed area. The participants placed themselves around the pole and danced in a slow and solemn circle, while the rest of the tribe looked on. The dancers usually fasted throughout the ceremony, which could last until they went into a trance and experienced visions.

In their Sun Dances, the Sioux, the Mandan, and other tribes practiced self-torture. The dancers cut slits in the skin of their chests and inserted sticks. The sticks were attached to a string leading to the central pole. As the dancers moved, they pulled against the strings until the sticks tore from their skin. The longer a dancer could endure the pain, the more honor and respect he would receive and the more blessings would come to the tribe.

▲ Dances played an important part in the ceremonial life
of the Plains Indians. In this photo a Sioux man wears
his ceremonial dance costume. His hair is adorned with
feathers and a roach.

THE SUN DANCE

The ritual of the Sun Dance was common to nearly all the Plains tribes. The Sioux called the dance "wiwanyag wachipi," which means "looking at the sun." The Sun Dance was held in the summer when the tribes came together to hunt buffalo. The Sun Dance was surrounded by elaborate ritual, which included prayers, chants, and dances. With rawhide thongs attached to their bodies and tied to poles, the dancers circled around, letting the thongs tear their flesh. The pain they endured signified their sacrifice for the good of the tribe. The entire ceremony usually lasted eight to 12 days. In this photograph, Ponca Indians, with streaming banners, gather in a semicircle to perform their Sun Dance.

The Kiowa Sun Dance was an elaborate affair in which a special stone carved in the form of a human was the central figure. Through this figure, the dancers would receive special spiritual powers. A large lodge was built for the dancers and before the ritual began, the people held a Buffalo Dance. After the dance, the young men who had vowed to do the Sun Dance entered the lodge. There they gazed on the sacred stone, which hung from the central pole of the lodge. For four days and nights, they danced and fasted. They sought strength for themselves in the hunt, in war, or often on behalf of a sick person or to bring many buffalo to the people. After the ceremony, the dancers rested in their own tepees while the rest of the people held a large feast.

OTHER CEREMONIES

The Plains Indians surrounded themselves with ceremonies. They had special rituals to bring the buffalo and to give them victory in war. They celebrated the renewal of life in the spring and

▲ Modern Plains Indians enjoy getting together for powwows. These events are an opportunity for the people to gather and celebrate their culture and heritage. In South Dakota, the Sioux perform traditional dances wearing ceremonial dress decorated in a variety of ways. Costumes are adorned with furs, fringe, beads, feathers, and often ribbons and bells. Some dancers wear bustles of feathers attached to their waists at the back.

performed dances and songs to aid in the healing of the sick or wounded.

All the tribes had some form of a Buffalo Dance, in which the dancers performed both the role of the buffalo and that of the hunter. Among the Mandan, a woman's society, called the Mandan Female White Buffalo Society, held special dances to call the buffalo to their territory.

The Cheyenne had a hunting ritual called the Animal Dance. According to tradition, it was taught to their hero, Sweet Medicine, by the chief spirit. In this ceremony, which lasted for five days, some of the men dressed as animals while others pretended to hunt them, herding them into a corral.

▲ Plains Indians did not always build scaffolds to hold their dead. Here, the corpse of an Oglala Sioux has been placed in a tree. Often, a warrior's shield, lance, and bow and arrows were hung from the burial scaffold to assist him in the other world.

Until the early 1800s, the Pawnee practiced human sacrifice as a ritual of renewal. The ceremony was called the Morning Star rite, and it was part of the Pawnee cult that worshiped the stars. In the ritual, a captive maiden, who represented the morning star and was considered sacred, was sacrificed just as the morning star rose in the sky. Tied to a scaffold she was shot with an arrow while at the same time she was struck on the head by a club. Her heart was then cut out and given as a sacrifice to the star.

This cruel rite stopped when in the early 1800s, so the story goes, a courageous Pawnee warrior rescued the young captive, who was a Cheyenne maiden. He cut her down from the scaffold at the last minute and carried her off on his horse, setting her free in Cheyenne territory. Since he was a warrior and hunter, he was revered for his bravery, and the practice of human sacrifice was dropped.

Death too was a cause for ceremony. Usually when a warrior died, his body was wrapped in robes and, along with his personal belongings, was placed on a high scaffold near the camp. Later, when the body had decomposed, it was buried in the ground. Among some tribes, the body was left on the scaffold. To honor the dead, a tribe would gather together and hold the Festival of the Dead. The deeds of the deceased were recounted, speeches were made, and songs were sung. Although some chants were mournful, the people believed that the dead had gone to another life in which there was no sadness or hardship. They also believed that the spirit of a brave person lived in the other world at the same age as when he died. Therefore there was no need to be sad when a young warrior died in battle.

LAWS

The Plains Indians did not depend on written laws to govern themselves. Their society was open and democratic, and maintaining order depended a great deal on an individual following his or her own conscience. It also depended on public opinion and on discipline imposed by special societies within the tribe, such as the Dog Soldier Society, which governed the rules and regulations of the hunt.

Chiefs were great warriors or especially skilled hunters, and they were venerated and respected. But they did not have the authority to give orders. The men met in council and discussed tribal matters, each giving his opinion about what the tribe should do. When a matter was decided, the force of public opinion and the stature of the council was more than enough to carry out the decision.

Stealing the horses of another tribe or killing an enemy in battle were considered brave deeds. But stealing from or murdering a member of one's own tribe was a grave crime. Among some tribes, such as the Cheyenne, a murderer was exiled, sent out alone for as long as 10 years before he or she could return. Among the Crow, a killer was expected to make compensation to the family of the victim, often taking care of the family for life. The Blackfoot used public mockery as a punishment for a wrongdoer. The people could make life so miserable for a person that he or she would be forced to leave the tribe.

TRIBAL SOCIETIES

Most of the Plains tribes were organized into societies, some of which were military and some of which were religious or were responsible for healing ceremonies. Every society had its own special dances, songs, medicine bundles, and costumes. Some societies were open to all males. For example, all Blackfoot men were organized into warrior groups according to their age. Many societies, especially the military ones, were closed. A warrior was invited to join based on his courageous actions in battle. Membership in such a society was considered an honor and earned a warrior great respect.

The Dog Soldier Society was common to most

▲ A Blackfoot man wears a buffalo-horn headdress and an elaborate dance costume in this photo from 1900.

Plains tribes. Members of this society policed the hunt, making sure it was properly organized and carried out, and led the other warriors in battle. Members of the Dog Soldier Society were chosen for their bravery and ability as warriors. They were expected to show great courage and daring in warfare. Among the Kiowa, the Dog Soldier Society was limited to 10 of the bravest warriors. When they went into battle, the leader of the society wore a special sash. He would ride out ahead of the others, dismount, and fasten one

▲ This depiction of a dancer of the Hidatsa Dog Soldier
Society was done in 1834. The Hidatsa were a farming
tribe who shared the upper Missouri River region with
the Mandan.

▲ These Mandan women dance to lure the buffalo. Their white hats, made from the hides of female buffalo, signify their membership in the Female White Buffalo Society. The women move slowly in a circle to the rhythm of a chanting chorus.

end of his sash to the ground by driving his lance through it. During the battle, no matter what happened, this warrior would stay anchored to his spot, fighting any enemy that came near him and urging on his companions. He would not leave the spot until another member of the society came to remove the lance.

Among the Crow, certain men were chosen as members of the Tobacco Society. Only they could plant the sacred tobacco and conduct the religious tobacco ceremony to bring power to the tribe as a whole.

Women too could belong to societies. Among the Mandan and Hidatsa, for example, women were members of the Female White Buffalo Society. The dances the women performed were meant to attract the buffalo to the hunters. Since the well-being of the entire tribe depended on

successful buffalo hunts, the Female White Buffalo Society was very important. Only the most respected women were allowed to join.

To the Plains Indians generosity and hospitality were among the greatest of virtues. Caring for the poor and sharing with the needy was the mark of a great person. A man who gave his favorite horse to a poor member of the tribe earned the highest respect. And it was mandatory to treat visitors openhandedly, with feasts and special ceremonies.

SPIRITUAL BELIEFS

❖ • ❖ • ❖ • ❖ • ❖ • ❖ • ❖ • ❖ • ❖ • ❖ • ❖ • ❖

SACRED SITES

▼ Devil's Tower in Wyoming is an unusual rock formation that rises 365 feet above the Plains. The site is sacred to the Sioux. President Theodore Roosevelt designated it the nation's first national monument in 1906.

❖ • ❖ • ❖ • ❖ • ❖ • ❖ • ❖ • ❖ • ❖ • ❖ • ❖

▶ The pieces of colored cloth that decorate this fence around a medicine wheel are there to bring good fortune to the Indian people who visit the site.

▼ Some experts think this circular ceremonial site, known as a medicine wheel, in the Bighorn Mountains of Wyoming dates back to around 1700. According to stories told by Kiowa, whose original homeland was in Wyoming, the medicine wheel was fashioned as part of the Sun Dance they celebrated with their Crow allies. The wheel is made of boulders with 28 spokes radiating from its central hub. It is 70 feet in diameter.

▲ The Black Hills of South Dakota are the spiritual home
of the Cheyenne.

▲ This Native American man in traditional dress was photographed at the Custer Battlefield National Monument in Montana. The battlefield itself is on the Crow Indian reservation, where each year the Crow hold ceremonial dances, rodeos, and other festivities.

CEREMONIAL DANCES AND OBJECTS

▲ A modern Native American performs a ceremonial dance. He holds a traditional stone-headed battle club.

◀ Dancing was an important part of Plains ceremonial life. This photo shows a Sioux drum with paintings on the head.

▼ This group carries on the tradition of their ancestors by performing the Eagle Feather Dance. Among the Plains Indians the eagle was venerated for its courage and power. Most tribes had an Eagle Society, and cere-monies, songs, and dances were performed to honor this great bird.

❖ • ❖ • ❖ • ❖ • ❖ • ❖ • ❖ • ❖ • ❖ • ❖

▲ A dancer at an Indian powwow in Nebraska performs
in a beautifully feathered costume.

▲ In 1888 many Plains Indians began practicing a new religion called the Ghost Dance. Special decorated shirts were worn by the dancers. This shirt, made of buckskin, was worn by an Arapaho. The front, shown here, and back have different designs.

CHAPTER FOUR

❖ • ❖ • ❖ • ❖ • ❖ • ❖ • ❖ • ❖ • ❖ • ❖ • ❖ • ❖

CHANGE

Among the first Europeans to see the Plains Indians was the Spanish explorer Francisco de Coronado. Heading an expedition from Mexico in 1540, he marched north into what is now the American Southwest. Coronado was searching for the mythical cities of gold that the Spaniards thought existed somewhere to the north. What Coronado found were the adobe villages of the Zuni Indians of what is now New Mexico. Coronado and his expedition then wandered eastward onto the Plains, still searching vainly for the cities of gold.

Instead, Coronado came upon villages of people who lived in "skin tents" and hunted "wild cows." When the explorer finally reached the Plains of Kansas and the grass-covered huts of the Wichita and no golden city had materialized, he gave up and returned to Mexico. There, Coronado reported that the land was useless, occupied only by primitive Indians and humpbacked cattle.

For more than another hundred years, the people of the prairies and Plains were left much to themselves. However, by the late 17th century,

Europeans were becoming more familiar with the western Indians. French fur traders and explorers from Canada ventured into the area of the upper Mississippi where they met Sioux and other Indian groups. The French explorer Robert de La Salle reported that a group of Cheyenne visited his fort in Illinois in 1682. Other French explorers drifted down the Mississippi River, observing the people along its banks and fur trading with them.

In the 1700s, trappers and hunters crossed the northern Plains to the mountains of the West, passing among the tribes of the prairies and Plains. In the southern Plains, Spanish settlers traded with the Indians and fought them when they attacked their settlements for horses. But it was not until the early 19th century that whites began to record in detail the unique way of life of the Plains Indians.

In 1803, the young United States bought from France the vast territory called Louisiana. Stretching from the Mississippi to the far Pacific Ocean, it encompassed the rich prairie grasslands and most of the Great Plains. Now the territories of the Plains Indians were of interest to the expanding nation and its settlers eager for land.

73

▲ The artist Samuel Seymour recorded this Pawnee gathering in 1819, when the Indians met with Major Stephen Long near Council Bluffs, Iowa. It is the earliest known picture of a gathering of Pawnee.

First, the farmer-hunters of the prairies felt the impact of settlement; soon after, the hunters of the Great Plains saw their lands transformed into farms, ranches, and towns.

THE FATE OF THE PRAIRIE FARMERS

Immediately after the purchase of Louisiana in 1803, the explorers Meriwether Lewis and William Clark set out on their journey across the prairies and Plains and mountains to the Pacific. The record of their expedition—the land and animals they saw, and the people they encountered—inspired pioneers to push farther and farther west.

First to come were the traders, who set up posts and exchanged guns, tools, blankets, and eventually alcohol for furs. They were soon followed by settlers eager to farm the rich soil of the prairies. Through treaties, Indians were persuaded to give up parts of their land, with promises that no more would be taken. For the most part, the treaties were not kept, and the flood of settlers onto the prairies overwhelmed the Indians. With little restraint from the government, settlers attacked the Indians, killed off the game they depended on, and took their land.

In addition to their superior weapons and their numbers, whites brought diseases that were unknown to the Indians and to which they had little resistance. Smallpox and cholera decimated the prairie tribes. By 1840 the once great Mandan were reduced to a remnant of about 150 people.

Indians who remained were then forced to move to the so-called Indian Territory, in what is now Oklahoma. In the mid-19th century, it was considered useless land. There the Indians lived on reservations, no longer able to farm or hunt and dependent on the government to give them food and shelter.

TAKING OVER THE GREAT PLAINS

Until the 1840s and 1850s, the Indians of the Great Plains were left in relative peace. Plains Indians had traded with fur trappers, the mountain men who traveled through their lands to the

Rockies. These early contacts were generally peaceful. Then, in the mid-1800s, wagon trains began rolling through the Plains on their way to California and Oregon. Soon, the government set up forts along the trails and sent soldiers to protect the pioneers as they passed through the Indians' land. Through a treaty signed in 1851, the Cheyenne and Arapaho agreed to the passage of settlers through their lands, with the condition that the Indians still retained all rights to hold their territory.

It was not long, however, before whites simply began to take over the land in violation of the treaty. They had discovered that the land was not the "desert" they had thought it was. Ranchers could raise cattle on the short grass, and the recently invented steel plow could cut through the tough sod and plow it into farmland. In addition, the skins of buffalo came to be in great demand in the East as "buffalo robes," which were used against the cold of open wagons and carriages. Hordes of buffalo hunters appeared on the Plains and began to slaughter the herds.

WAR ON THE PLAINS

When the Indians fought back, a series of wars broke out that lasted until the end of the 19th

THE SLAUGHTER OF THE BUFFALO

In 1850, about 20 million buffalo still roamed the Plains. By 1889, authorities could count only 551 survivors. The incredible slaughter of the buffalo began in earnest after the Civil War ended in 1865. First, settlers on the Plains plowed under the grass that the herds depended on for food. Then, as merchants demanded more and more buffalo hides and railroad companies pushing westward wanted meat for their workers, professional hunters swarmed onto the Plains, slaughtering the beasts by the millions. William "Buffalo Bill" Cody claimed he killed 4,000 buffalo in only 18 months. Although the buffalo he killed were used to feed railway workers, in general the killing was excessive and wasteful. Hunters who wanted only the hides left the meat to rot. For sport, peo

ple crossing the Plains by train shot the animals indiscriminately, as in the drawing shown here.

Deliberately deprived of the source of their food, clothing, and shelter, the Indians finally had little choice but to move to the reservations, where they were dependent on government supplies.

LEADERS OF DISTINCTION

QUANAH PARKER

In Comanche, his first name, Quanah, means fragrant, or sweet-smelling. His last name is an English name, for his mother, Cynthia Ann Parker, was a white Texas woman, abducted as a child by the Comanche and adopted into their tribe. Quanah was around 15 when in 1860, his mother, against her wishes, was retaken by Texas Rangers in a raid on their village. Not until years later did Quanah learn that his mother, separated from her husband and children and grieving for the people she thought of as her own, starved herself to death. When his father was killed and his younger brother died, Quanah joined the Kwahadie band of Comanche, who lived in the remote, desolate Staked Plains of the Texas Panhandle. From there, the tall, black-haired young man, with his gray-blue eyes and black war paint, led his band of warriors in swift attacks on army posts—and then vanished into the Panhandle. When other Comanche signed the Treaty of Medicine Lodge Creek in 1867, Quanah refused: "Let the white chiefs know that the Kwahadie are warriors," he said. "We'll surrender when the blue-coats come and whip us on the Staked Plains." The soldiers did penetrate into the Staked Plains, and for nearly 10 years pursued Quanah and his band. In scores of raids and skirmishes, the cavalry finally wore down the Kwahadie. In 1875, Quanah and his band surrendered. They were the last band of Indians to surrender on the southern Plains. Until his death in 1911, Quanah Parker lived on the reservation. He became the Comanche's principal chief—now a man of peace rather than war. He protected the interests of his people by fighting with government officials to save reservation lands. He brought money to the reservation by leasing some its land to Texas cattle ranchers. Quanah served as a deputy sheriff in Lawton, Oklahoma, and the town of Quanah, Texas, is named for him.

CRAZY HORSE

Crazy Horse (Tashunka Witco in Sioux) was one of the most daring of the Sioux chiefs. In a vision he had as a young man in the 1850s, he saw himself with trailing, unbraided hair, adorned with the feather of a red hawk, and with a smooth stone behind his ear. Thereafter he went into battle dressed this way. Although his life was short—he was born around 1841 and died in 1877—he fought in all the major battles of the Sioux to protect their sacred Black Hills. His most famous battle was that at the Little Big Horn when, as war chief of the Oglala Sioux, he and his Cheyenne allies wiped out Custer and his troops. But it was his last great battle. Pursued by the army, he and about 1,000 Sioux surrendered in 1877. He and his people were promised land in the Powder River country. Crazy Horse felt other chiefs had become weak and surrendered to the white man's way. Arguments between him and older chiefs, and the authorities' fear of Crazy Horse as a potential leader of rebellion, brought his downfall. In August 1877, Crazy Horse tried to make his way to the Powder River country but was captured by troops. As his guards herded him toward a prison barracks, he realized he was to be confined, perhaps for the rest of his life. Crazy Horse struggled with the guards, and in the melee, a guard bayoneted him. Dying, he asked that his heart be returned to the Powder River country. No one knows where his body lies, for his parents took it and disappeared. Legend has it that they buried his remains near Wounded Knee.

SATANTA

Like the Comanche, and the Sioux, the Kiowa resisted the invasion of whites. Their war leader, Satanta, led them in their struggle. An imposing man, over 6 feet tall, he was also known as a great orator. Despite his feelings of sorrow, Satanta signed the treaty of Medicine Lodge Creek and agreed to live on the reservation. However, when the promises of the treaty were not kept, Satanta rebelled and began leading raids into Texas. Following a raid in 1871, Satanta boldly admitted he had led his warriors in defiance of the authorities. He spent two years in prison, and at his release vowed to abandon war against the whites. But hostilities broke out again as angry Kiowa left the reservation to strike at buffalo hunters, army posts, and settlements. Although Satanta declared he was not involved, he was once again arrested and sentenced to life in prison. Satanta could not live in a jail. In September, 1878, at the age of 58, he flung himself from a window of the prison hospital.

▲ This photograph, taken in 1868, shows General William Tecumseh Sherman and Sioux leaders signing the Treaty of Fort Laramie.

century. The government made more treaties with the tribes, but when settlers wanted more land or when miners found gold, the treaties were broken. In 1859, gold was discovered in eastern Colorado, on the lands of the Cheyenne and the Arapaho. Prospectors poured into the Indians' hunting grounds, digging up the land and scattering the buffalo herds. When the tribes refused to sell their lands for mining, the army attacked Indian villages and deliberately slaughtered the buffalo. The Cheyenne and Arapaho retaliated by raiding wagon trains, settlements, and army posts.

Finally in 1864, the military commander of the area, Colonel John Chivington, suggested a meeting at which he promised that the war would be over and the tribes safe from attack if the Indians would simply report to the army post at Fort Lyon, Colorado. In November, Cheyenne leaders Black Kettle and White Antelope surrendered their band at a place called Sand Creek. Disregarding the white flag raised by Black Kettle, Chivington attacked with rifles and cannon fire. Black Kettle and some warriors managed to escape, but when the firing was over, some 200

Indians—half of them women and children—were dead.

Word of the massacre at Sand Creek spread, and war flared. In two major campaigns in the northern and southern Plains, the army attempted to drive the tribes onto reservations. Some tribes agreed, but in the north, the Sioux under Red Cloud refused. The Sioux continued to attack army posts and wagon trains coming into their lands. In the southern Plains, the Cheyenne and Arapaho also kept up their attacks on railroads, mining camps, and army posts.

Failing to dislodge the tribes, the government finally concluded two treaties. Through the Treaty of Medicine Lodge Creek in 1867, the southern Cheyenne and Arapaho and the Kiowa and Comanche were to give up their traditional lands and settle on reservations in Indian Territory. However, they would be allowed to hunt on their former lands in Kansas and Texas. On the

▲ This photograph of Chief Sitting Bull was taken around 1885. His Indian name, Tatanka Yotanka, actually means Sitting Buffalo. Historians consider him one of the most dedicated and able Plains leaders.

reservations, the government would provide them with food and other supplies. The government negotiator for the treaty was William Tecumseh Sherman, the famous Union general of the Civil War. It was Sherman who had said that the Indians were "the enemies of our race and of our civilization." Sherman was determined to force the Indians onto the reservations, and he told the leaders of the tribes that they could not stop the advance of settlers, roads, and railroads. He reminded them of the government's great power to destroy all the tribes. In the end, with some exceptions, the chiefs signed the treaty.

In the northern Plains, the government negotiated with the Sioux and their northern Cheyenne allies, who were resisting the incursion of whites into their traditional hunting grounds in Montana. In 1862, when gold was discovered north of the Platte River, miners and traders poured into Sioux lands. The Sioux fought so fiercely that the government decided to try and make peace rather than carry on a long war. The United States was then also engaged in fighting the Civil War

(1861–65). But it was not until 1868 that the Sioux agreed to a treaty, called the Treaty of Fort Laramie. By this time, the Sioux had forced the government to abandon forts in Indian lands and move out the soldiers. By the terms of the treaty, all the land west of the Missouri River in present-day South Dakota was to be a reservation for the Sioux. In addition, land west of the reservation, called the Powder River country, was to be forever Indian land. The treaty declared "No white person or persons shall be permitted to settle upon or occupy any portion of the [Powder River Country]; or without consent of the Indians . . . to pass through the same." Some chiefs refused to sign the treaty, among them Sitting Bull of the Hunkpapa Sioux. He and others did not go to the reservation land but set up their villages in the Powder River country.

In spite of treaties, the wars did not stop. Whites continued to settle in Indian lands and move in ever greater numbers over the trails to the west that led through the Indian nations. The government ignored the provisions of the treaties. Betrayed by the government, angry and frustrated, hundreds of Indians left the reservations, forming bands and joining with other Indians who had not signed the treaties.

Conflict continued on the northern and southern Plains, with raids and attacks by the Indians and retaliation by the army. Then, in the late 1860s, the army launched full-scale warfare against the Plains tribes. At the same time, the government decided that no Indian tribe would ever again be considered an independent nation and went on to encourage settlers to continue the slaughter of the buffalo. Although some bands of Cheyenne, Comanche, Arapaho, and Kiowa still fought on, a series of losing battles in the northern and southern Plains broke the major Indian resistance.

As the army kept up its pressure, more and more Indians were herded onto reservations. But it was not over yet, for the Sioux in the north still hung onto their ancestral lands.

BATTLE OF THE LITTLE BIG HORN

In 1874, gold was discovered in the sacred land of the Sioux in the Black Hills of the Dakota Territory. Once again, the authorities tried to force the Indians to sell their rights. They refused and took a stand in what became perhaps the most famous conflict of the Indian wars—the Battle of the Little Big Horn in southern Montana in 1876.

In May of that year, Lieutenant Colonel George Armstrong Custer led a force of about 250 soldiers of the United States Seventh Cavalry out from Fort Abraham Lincoln in the Dakota Territory. His mission was to search out bands of Sioux and force them onto reservations.

For a month, Custer's force rode across the Plains without seeing the Indians. Then on June 25, he came to the Little Big Horn River, where he spotted an encampment of Sioux and Cheyenne, who had never surrendered. The camp numbered some 7,000 people. However, Custer was unaware of the Indians' strength because bluffs along the river hid most of the village from sight.

Custer sent one contingent of soldiers to scout the land and another force to cross the river and attack the village. The attackers were driven back across the river, where they dug in to carry on the fight. In the meantime, a force of Sioux and Cheyenne, under chiefs Sitting Bull and Crazy Horse, surrounded Custer and his remaining men. In the matter of an hour or so, the battle was over. Custer and all the soldiers with him were killed. Those who had dug in along the river bank fought on for another day, when suddenly the Indians broke off the fight. Their scouts had reported that another army force was fast approaching.

THE FINAL RESISTANCE

The defeat of Custer shocked and angered the entire nation. Now the government was determined to drive the Indians from the Plains. The army set out to hunt them down, following and capturing the bands one by one. Chief Sitting Bull escaped to Canada, but returned later in 1881, surrendering peacefully. Crazy Horse fought on for two years, but finally surrendered in 1877 and was killed by soldiers when it was thought he was trying to escape.

The Cheyenne had been driven to reservations in Oklahoma, but in 1878, they broke away and under their leader Dull Knife, began to trek northward to their hunting grounds in Montana. They suffered great hardship, and for a time eluded the pursuing army. In the end, they were overtaken and scores were killed before the rest surrendered. By 1881, the last of the Plains tribes had been exiled to reservations.

Yet there was still a brief conflict to come. With everything gone, the Indians turned to their

▲ Kicking Bear, a medicine man, was one of the leaders of the Sioux Ghost Dance movement. He believed that special Ghost Dance shirts could stop bullets.

visions through the Ghost Dance. This religion had originated with a Paiute Indian in Nevada named Wovoka, who declared that an Indian messiah would appear who would reawaken the dead, bring back the buffalo, and cause the whites to disappear. Wovoka also preached peace and nonviolence. The events Wovoka predicted would occur through prayer, avoidance of the ways of whites—especially the use of alcohol—and a special dance called the Ghost Dance, during which the participants gained visions and talked with the dead. Some members of the Ghost Dance religion also believed that when they wore special Ghost Shirts they were invulnerable to bullets.

The Ghost Dance religion spread quickly to the Plains Indian reservations. As the movement gained more and more followers, the authorities became frightened. Not knowing that the religion taught nonviolence, they concluded that it was a war dance and possibly a prelude to an Indian uprising. They decided to stamp it out.

The end came in December 1890. Army troops

▲ In the last conflict of the Plains wars, Chief Big Foot and most of his band were shot down at Wounded Knee Creek. The soldiers who did the killing were from units of Colonel Custer's famous Seventh Cavalry. This grisly photograph shows Big Foot frozen in death on the site of the massacre. He and the other dead were later buried in a mass grave.

were sent to Pine Ridge and Rosebud reservations in South Dakota to stop the dancing. A large Ghost Dance was planned in protest, and the dancers asked Chief Sitting Bull to join them. Sitting Bull was a respected religious leader among his people, and although he did not believe all of the tenets of the Ghost Dance religion, he did not discourage his people from practicing it. When the alarmed authorities tried to arrest Sitting Bull on the reservation, a group of Ghost Dancers protested. In the scuffle that followed, Sitting Bull was shot and killed.

The news of his death spread quickly, and many Indians, fearful for their lives, fled from the reservations. Followed by pursuing soldiers, one band of Sioux, led by Big Foot, surrendered on December 28. Big Foot had been a Ghost Dance leader but now wanted peace instead—he

was leading his people to Pine Ridge, not to the site where the Ghost Dance was being held. Soldiers marched the people to an army camp at a place called Wounded Knee Creek. Here, the Indians were counted: 120 men and 230 women. The commander posted guards for the night and set up several small cannons around the camp.

In the morning, the soldiers began searching for weapons. As they tried to disarm the Indians, one, named Black Coyote, raised his rifle above his head, declaring he would not give it up. Then a shot was fired. Whether or not it was Black Coyote, no one really knows, but it was a signal for the soldiers to open fire. Rifles and pistols blazed as groups of Indians fought back with knives and clubs. Then the cannons began to fire, and as the people fled, they were cut down by the big guns. When the massacre was over, Big Foot and possibly as many as 300 men, women, and children were dead. Some bodies of women and children were found as far as two miles from the camp, indicating that the soldiers had deliberately hunted them down.

The soldiers piled the remaining people into wagons and headed them toward the Pine Ridge reservation. Since a blizzard was approaching, the soldiers left the dead. Later, a burial party re-

turned to Wounded Knee Creek to find the bodies of the dead frozen where they had fallen.

INDIAN RESERVATIONS

The massacre at Wounded Knee was the end of the Indians' battles for the Great Plains. Their remnants were confined to reservations, under the authority of the Bureau of Indian Affairs. This government agency had been set up as early as 1824 as part of the War Department. Its purpose was to oversee trade with Indians and to take charge of the removal and settlement of Indians to reservations. In 1849, the bureau had become part of the Department of the Interior, where it remains today.

The idea behind reservations was to break the tribal ways and turn the Indians into whites, or assimilate them. In the process, Indian ideas, traditions, values—their entire culture—was to be erased and that of the whites imposed. And of course, there were the former Indian lands to be turned into farms and ranches and the minerals beneath the soil to be exploited.

On reservations, the Indians' religious and tribal customs were forbidden. They could not hunt for food but had to depend on rations

▲ On the reservations, Indians set up tepee camps. This photograph, taken in 1890, shows a Sioux camp on the Pine Ridge reservation, where in that same year Chief Sitting Bull was killed. Although the Indians did not retaliate for Sitting Bull's death, they were relentlessly pursued by the army in its attempt to crush the Ghost Dance.

handed out by the reservation agency. In many cases, the people in charge of the reservations were corrupt, stealing the funds for food and clothing. Entirely dependent on the government, the Indians' existence was aimless and without hope.

Descriptions of life on the reservations did shock reformers, and the government passed some laws to alleviate the conditions. One was the Dawes Act of 1887, through which some Indian tribal lands were given to individual families to farm. This too was an attempt to make the Indians into whites. But the idea of individual ownership of land was totally foreign to the Plains Indians. Traditionally, no one Indian owned a piece of land; it belonged to all of them. Furthermore, the Plains Indians were not farmers, and much of the land was barely suited for

▲ Chief Sitting Bull poses with William F. Cody, better
known as Buffalo Bill because he became famous as a
buffalo hunter. Cody organized a Wild West show in
1883, and some chiefs, like Sitting Bull, toured with the
show. Despite the seeming indignity of their roles, they
used the show to mock and debunk whites' ideas of the
"wild west."

▲ In an attempt to bring the plight of Indians to the attention of the government, Sioux and Crow leaders meet with President Warren G. Harding (center) in 1921 at the White House in Washington, D.C.

individual farming anyway. The plan failed.

In addition, many of the remaining reservation lands were opened up for sale to whites. This was in spite of treaties which had promised that the reservations, bad as they were, were still Indian lands.

By the early 20th century, the Plains Indians were enduring chronic poverty. The farming plan had not worked and much reservation land had been lost to white ownership. In the 1930s, through the Indian Reorganization Act, the government stopped non-Indian ownership of tribal lands and opened up for the Indians reservation lands that had not yet been taken over by whites. The government offered low-cost loans and urged the Indians to organize as tribes to renew their ancestral lands.

The program did help the Indians. Now, working through tribal councils and with government sponsorship, they were in charge of their tribal affairs. However, the federal government still held reservation land in trust for the Indians. This means that the government over-

sees the land—it cannot be bought, sold, leased, rented or its resources used without agreement between the government and the Indians.

Under the Reorganization Act, Indian traditions, ceremonies, religions, and crafts were encouraged. Many Indian children attended public schools, government-run Indian colleges were established, and health facilities improved. The Indians, with the help of the government, were making a comeback, showing that with encouragement they could help themselves.

Then, in the 1950s, the government reversed itself. With the idea in mind that the government should not be giving what it considered handouts, programs of loans and credit were stopped. Indians were encouraged to leave their lands and get jobs elsewhere. The idea of tribal groups and

▲ This young Indian man wears a feathered bonnet with trailing pieces of fur at a powwow in Wyoming.

communities working together was dumped. The government sought to take away its protection and services and began a policy of dissolving, or terminating, the tribes.

The termination plan was never completely implemented, although tribes in California, Oregon, and Wisconsin were terminated. By the end of the 1950s, the government returned once again to its policy of overseeing and helping the Indians. However, the government does not feed or clothe Indians nor does it give them pensions, as many people believe. And when Indians leave the reservations, they are on their own, like everyone else. Indians are citizens of the United States. They vote, travel freely as they wish, and pay taxes as do all citizens. The exception to tax paying involves reservation lands. Income that Indians gain from their use of reservation land is free from taxes. If an Indian businessperson sets up a shop on a reservation to sell crafts and other products to visitors, the income from those sales is not taxed.

The largest Sioux reservations today are in South Dakota, although there is a Sioux and Assiniboine reservation in Montana. The Crow, the Blackfoot, and the Cheyenne also have reservations in Montana. There is a Cheyenne reservation as well in Oklahoma, along with Arapaho, Kiowa, and Comanche reservations. Today, the Plains tribes are mostly farmers and ranchers. In spite of improvements in health care and education, they are, however, still among the poorest of American minorities.

Although in theory they govern themselves through tribal councils, in practice the federal government still has authority to make many decisions regarding Indian affairs, such as the use of the land. A major problem between Indians and the government is their differing ideas of government and decision making. The Plains Indians had no concept of the notion of majority rule in which decisions are made based on what most of the people want and are then handed down by a leader or group of leaders. They governed themselves through an open and loose democracy in which no one chief or leader had total authority. Chiefs were not elected nor did they give orders. Decisions about war, peace, and the hunt were made by mutual consent among the most respected chiefs and warriors. Forcing the whites' ideas of government on Indians has brought conflict between the tribes and the government and within the tribes themselves. Many tribal members reject the idea of majority rule and the decision making of the tribal councils as non-Indian and as a way of forcing Indians into subservience to whites.

Among the people, conflict has arisen between the so-called modern Indians and the traditionalists. Some feel that they and their children must be more a part of white society if they are to get along in the modern world. Others insist that the old ways of language, beliefs, and customs be retained and that Indians must become more militant in their demands.

In the 1960s, in the decade of the civil rights movement and protests against the war in Vietnam, many Indians struggled for "Red Power." Probably the most activist and militant Indian organization is the American Indian Movement

(AIM). It was founded in 1968 by three Chippewa Indians, Dennis Banks, Clyde Bellecourt, and George Mitchell, and a Sioux, Russell Means. AIM's goals include more direct participation by Indians in decisions affecting their lives and less involvement by the government, especially the Bureau of Indian Affairs. AIM also feels that many tribal councils are too authoritarian and sometimes corrupt, making decisions that serve themselves and not the best interests of the entire tribe. AIM's way of dramatizing the plight of all American Indians was to occupy property held by the federal government.

In 1969 an AIM group took over Alcatraz Island in San Francisco Bay, the abandoned site of the former, and famous, Alcatraz prison. They held the island until 1971, when federal officials finally moved them out. In 1972, AIM marched on Washington and for six days occupied the offices of the Bureau of Indian Affairs.

However, the most dramatic confrontation took place in 1973, on the Pine Ridge Reservation in South Dakota, home to about 11,000 Sioux. It was especially significant for AIM because it occurred on the site of the 1890 massacre at Wounded Knee. Part of the reason for the so-called Siege of Wounded Knee came about because AIM members, led by Russell Means, were dissatisfied with the leadership of the tribal council, which AIM considered too subservient to the Bureau of Indian Affairs.

In February of 1973, AIM called for demonstrations to protest the stabbing of a young Sioux by a white man. The protests got out of hand, and the rebellious AIM members and their supporters took over some buildings in the village of Wounded Knee on the reservation. They armed themselves and set up roadblocks. Federal agents moved in, and for 71 days, the militants held out. Shooting incidents occurred between the Indians and the federal agents, killing two Indians and wounding a federal agent. There were cease fires and negotiations and more shooting.

Finally an agreement was reached and AIM leaders surrendered. Banks and Means were freed on bail and later tried in court. But the charges against them were finally dismissed on the grounds that the government prosecution had not conducted the case properly.

TODAY ON THE PLAINS

Today, despite the years of government policies of intervention or indifference, Plains Indians

▲ In 1973, at Wounded Knee, South Dakota, Indians placed a buffalo skull and peace pipes on the site of the earlier massacre. At left is the medicine man Crow Dog, who was also a leader of the American Indian Movement (AIM).

have not vanished. More than ever, they are speaking out to run their own affairs. In some communities they control their own schools and have established Indian community colleges. Sinte Gleska College (the Indian name for Spotted Tail, a 19th-century Sioux leader) was created by the Rosebud Sioux in South Dakota and is controlled by them.

Indians are also fighting to regain their treaty rights. The Sioux are still fighting through the courts to get back the land of their sacred Black Hills, taken from them in defiance of their treaty with the government. Although the government awarded the Sioux $105 million to settle their claim, it did not give back the Black Hills. The majority of Sioux want the land rather than the money.

The Plains Indians have also joined with other Native Americans in a number of organiza-

▲ Dixon Palmer, also known by his Kiowa/Choctaw
name of Blue Hail, is a noted contemporary tepee artist.

▲ Participants in a Sioux powwow display traditional headdresses. Deer-tail roaches and eagle feathers are worn by these three men.

tions to protect Indian rights. The Native American Rights Fund is a law group that protects Indian resources such as land, water, and mineral rights. One of the best known groups is the National Congress of American Indians. As a lobbying group, it tries to influence government policy on issues such as protecting Indian lands, resources, and culture. Uniting with other tribes, Plains Indians have formed a multitude of organizations that work together in many areas, including health, education, housing, and energy.

In the early 1900s, the United States government, which by then had removed most Indians to reservations, forbade the Sun Dance. The official reason given was that the dancers practiced self-torture. However, whether or not a tribe practiced self-torture, the ceremony was still forbidden, as part of the government's suppression of Indian religion. Not until the 1930s were the Indians given the same religious freedom as other Americans, at which time the Sun Dance was revived. It is practiced today among Indians of the Plains. In 1967, for instance, the Sioux

held a Sun Dance in Winner, South Dakota. The procession, the dancing, the prayers, the piercing of the dancers' flesh were the traditional rituals of the people's ancestors. The purpose of the Sun Dance was to offer prayers for peace among all people and to protect from harm the Sioux men who were fighting in the Vietnam War.

An important expression of Plains Indians' togetherness is the powwow, an occasion for Indians of several different tribes to gather and dance, feast, sing, and meet with one another. Blackfoot, Crow, Sioux, and other Plains tribes keep alive their traditions and heritages through the powwows.

In the arts—painting, music, the theater, literature—the Indians of the Plains and prairies have enriched the lives of all Americans. The Osage Maria Tallchief was the first American ballet dancer to appear at the Bolshoi Theater in Moscow. Vine Deloria, Jr., a Sioux, wrote about and for the Plains Indians in his book *Custer Died for Your Sins*. N. Scott Momaday, a Kiowa poet and novelist, won the 1969 Pulitzer Prize for Literature for his novel *House Made of Dawn*. Traditionally, the Plains Indians created unique paintings, which told their history and their ways of life. They continue to depict their ways of life in contemporary art. Alvin Jake, a Pawnee artist, has created scenes of everyday life among his people. Kiowa artists Sharron Ahtone Harjo and Robert Redbird continue the Kiowa's artistic traditions through their paintings, which memorialize the history and heritage of their people.

From their early beginnings, their migrations, and their lives of freedom on the Great Plains through resistance, wars, and final deprivation and dislocation, the Indians of the Plains are entering a new era in which they can find hope for their future. Perhaps what lies ahead for the Plains people can be expressed in the words of a song chanted in the sweat lodges:

> A voice I will send,
> hear me,
> the land all over
> a voice I am sending,
> hear me.
> I will live.
> I will live.

MODELN LIFE

❖ • ❖ • ❖ • ❖ • ❖ • ❖ • ❖ • ❖ • ❖ • ❖ • ❖

A PROUD HERITAGE

◀ A well-known aspect of Indian culture is expressed through these colorful U.S. postage stamps depicting the traditional headdresses of Plains tribes.

▼ This gigantic contemporary sculpture in South Dakota's Black Hills is a memorial to Crazy Horse. No photographs of Crazy Horse were ever taken, and no artist ever painted him.

❖ • ❖ • ❖ • ❖ • ❖ • ❖ • ❖ • ❖ • ❖ • ❖ • ❖

MODERN ARTISTS

▲ Using tennis shoes as a base Sioux craftswoman Imogene Goodshot has added beads to create a statement about the role of tradition in modern Indian life.

▲ An example of modern Sioux art in a traditional form is this doll, called "Sioux Woman," created by artist Rhonda Holy Bear.

POWWOWS

▶ These children are dressed in traditional ceremonial garb for a powwow in North Dakota.

▼ These mounted Indians are on parade as part of the annual Calgary Stampede, held each summer in Calgary, Alberta.

▲ One of the sights at the Calgary Stampede is this
Blackfoot Indian village.

▶ Indian dancers like this group are part of the many events that the state of Wyoming holds every summer to celebrate its Native American heritage.

▼ A throng of dancers performs at a powwow in North Dakota.

INDEX

PICTURE CREDITS

William H. Allen, Jr.: 41 top; Atlatl: 90, 91; Badlands National Park: 22 top and bottom; Betty Crowell: 92 bottom, 93; Custer Battlefield National Monument: 68; Kent and Donna Dannen: 20; Richard Day: 17; Denver Museum of Natural History, Photo Archives: 46, 47 top and bottom, 70 top, 72; Jeff Henry: 19 bottom, 66 top and bottom; Joseph and Arlene Johannets: 45; Knife River National Park: 42, 70 bottom; Library of Congress: 8, 11, 12, 14, 15, 16, 27, 28, 29, 30, 32, 33, 34, 37, 38, 39, 40 left and right, 51, 52, 53, 56, 57, 62, 63, 64, 74, 75, 80, 83, 84; Kevin Magee: 23; Robert and Linda Mitchell: 21 top; Montana Department of Commerce: 43, 48; National Archives: 3, 9, 10, 26, 31, 58-59, 61, 76-77, 78, 79, 81, 82; Nebraska Department of Economic Development: 69, 71; North Dakota Tourism: 92 top, 94 bottom; Jack Olson: 24, 89 bottom; Provincial Archives of Alberta, E. Brown Collection: 6; Chase Roe: 19 top; Sylvia Schlender: 41 bottom; Rob and Melissa Simpson: 18; South Dakota Tourism: 60, 88; UPI/Bettmann Newsphotos: 86; U.S. Department of the Interior, Indian Arts and Crafts Board, Southern Plains Indian Museum and Crafts Center: 35, 36, 87; U.S. Postal Service: 89 top; Steve Warble: 21 bottom, 65; George Wuerthner: 44, 67; Wyoming Travel Commission: 85, 94 top.